CW00468731

The Cairn Valley Light Railway

Moniaive to Dumfries

by
Ian Kirkpatrick

THE OAKWOOD PRESS

© Oakwood Press & Ian Kirkpatrick 2000

British Library Cataloguing in Publication Data
A Record for this book is available from the British Library
ISBN 0 85361 567 5

Typeset by Oakwood Graphics.
Repro by Ford Graphics, Ringwood, Hants.
Printed by Stour Print Ltd, Blandford Forum, Dorset.

Front cover
A period picture postcard showing a railmotor standing at Moniaive station during the early years of the Cairn Valley Light Railway.   *Author's Collection*

Rear cover
A 1907 map from the *Railway Clearing House Junction Diagram* book showing lines radiating from Dumfries.
Tickets from the LMS period. The ticket for ONE BICYCLE AND ONE SEAT conjures up idyllic images of exploring the Cairn Valley by bike and steam train.   *Author's Collection*

Published by The Oakwood Press (Usk), P.O. Box 13, Usk, Mon., NP15 1YS.
E-mail: oakwood-press@dial.pipex.com
Website: www.oakwood-press.dial.pipex.com

Contents

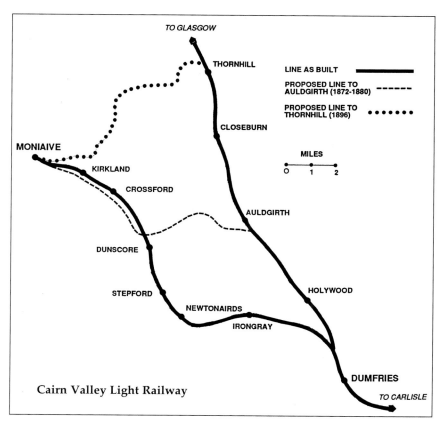

Cairn Valley Light Railway

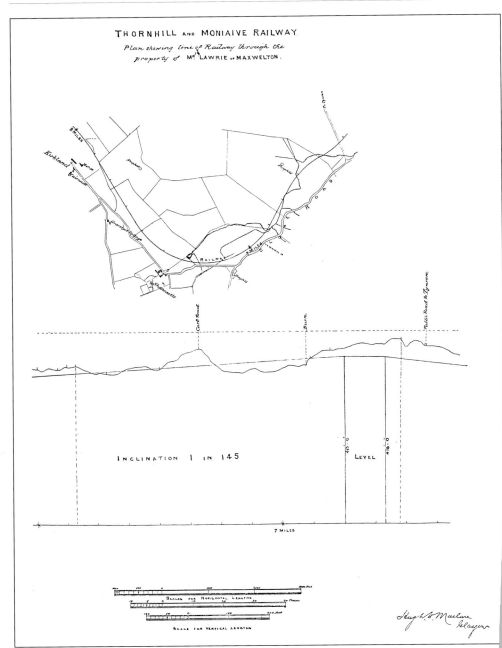

Part of the survey undertaken by Hugh Maclure in 1865 for a railway from Moniaive to Thornhill.
Author's Collection

Chapter One

First Proposals

Today it is hard to believe that a railway once ran by the secluded banks of the Cairn water, which flows between the village of Moniaive and the County town of Dumfries in South-West Scotland. But the Cairn Valley Light Railway did exist, although like many other rural branches it was short lived, opening in 1905 and closing barely 45 years later in the face of competition from the motor bus, car and lorry.

The terminus of the line, Moniaive in Glencairn Parish in North-West Dumfriesshire, is certainly an appealing place. A trim village on the old main road from Galloway to Edinburgh, its narrow streets of rose-fronted cottages and the surrounding countryside of rolling hills and tumbling burns have always proved inviting to visitors. Yet it would stretch even the most fertile imagination to consider that a railway would ever have been viable to such a quiet out-of-the-way spot along such a sparsely populated route.

The Cairn Valley line was one of the last to be built by its parent company, the Glasgow and South Western (G&SW) Railway, which by the beginning of the 20th century operated a fairly extensive network of feeder branches connecting the mining and market towns of Renfrewshire, Ayrshire, and Dumfriesshire with Glasgow or the South through Dumfries and Carlisle. However, the reason why the little branch to Moniaive ever existed was not some vision of a bright new age, but rather a late result of the 'railway mania' of the Victorian period when a rail connection was considered essential to ensure the economic and physical growth of any self-respecting town or village.

Indeed the first notice of any desire to extend a branch line to serve the agricultural area around Moniaive appeared as early as 4th January, 1865, when the *Dumfries and Galloway Standard* reported on a meeting of prominent local landowners and businessmen, 'for promoting a railway between Minnyhive, Penpont and the Glasgow and South Western Railway'.

The chairman of this meeting, Mr Samuel McCall of Caitloch, Moniaive, stated that the proprietors of the land needed for the proposed railway had agreed that a survey should be made between Moniaive and Thornhill station. It was then suggested that a committee should approach the G&SW Railway Company to arrange for this survey to be carried out. The *Standard's* report concluded that: 'The district around Minnyhive and Penpont is now heartily entering into the advantages and necessity of a railway, and with a strong and united effort there are no fears entertained of the result'.

On 17th January, 1865, the committee met with the Directors of the G&SW Company in Glasgow, where it was agreed that the railway promoters would pay for one-third of the cost of a preliminary survey and that the G&SW would pay for the remainder. Although Glasgow civil engineer Hugh Maclure duly carried out the survey, the *Standard's* report was over optimistic and on 9th January, 1866 the promoters informed the G&SW that they did not intend to proceed with the line.

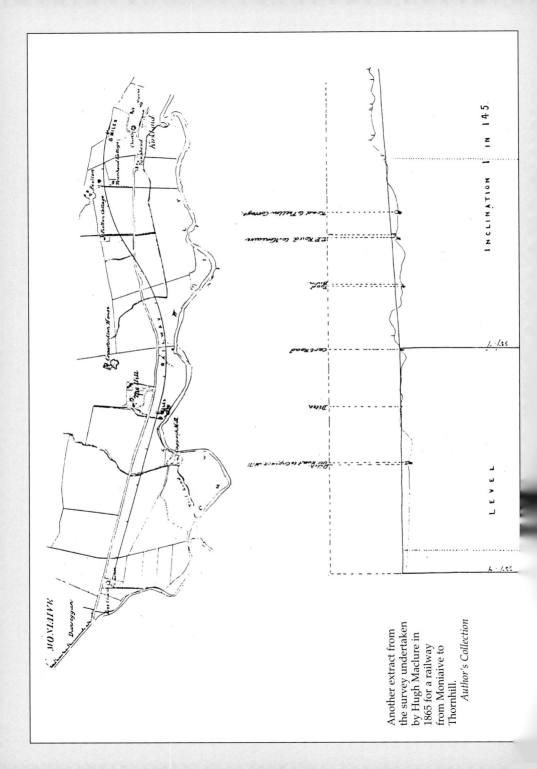

Another extract from
the survey undertaken
by Hugh Maclure in
1865 for a railway
from Moniaive to
Thornhill.

Author's Collection

However, in July 1866 the G&SW received a letter from Mr Christopher Harkness of Dumfries, requesting support for another Moniaive railway scheme. This time the proposed route was from Moniaive, down part of the Cairn Valley to Dunscore, and from there east to join the G&SW's main line near Auldgirth station. The letter included a report from an Edinburgh civil engineer, Mr Jopp, which estimated the cost of the line as £66,000. The Directors' reply to Mr Harkness pointed out that the railway would be of benefit mainly to its promoters, who therefore should be prepared to raise the necessary capital themselves; but the company also requested to see a list of subscribers to the line and a plan of its intended route.

In September 1866, the *Standard* reported on a meeting held in Dunscore to gauge support for the new railway. Mr Harkness read out a draft prospectus and exhibited a tracing of the line, as surveyed by Mr Jopp. He explained that the tracing had been submitted to Mr Johnston, manager of the G&SW, who approved of it in principle, but suggested that a fork junction should be made at the entrance to Auldgirth station, one branch to lead into the station and the other direct into the G&SW main line. Mr Harkness also referred to the support that the G&SW most likely would provide for the venture and read out a list of promised subscriptions, which amounted to nearly £10,000. A Mr James Dodds then addressed the meeting and provided more details of the scheme. A discussion followed, after which the Revd John Hope of Dunscore expressed great satisfaction with the given explanations. It was agreed unanimously to support the proposed railway and a committee was set up to seek further subscriptions.

By November, the amount pledged had grown to £17,130 and the *Standard* was confident that: 'We may soon expect now to see the Glasgow and South-Western Railway Company coming forward and manifesting such an interest to the concern (which will prove a productive one to them) as shall put it beyond the reach of danger'.

Again the paper was prematurely optimistic. In January 1867, Mr Harkness informed the G&SW that the subscriptions had grown to £20,150 and tried unsuccessfully to get the company to match this amount with a further £20,000. Over the next nine months, Mr Harkness continued to seek subscriptions from the G&SW. In every case these were refused and finally the scheme had to be abandoned

But the notion of running a line to Moniaive persisted and another meeting to discuss its possible construction was held there in October 1870. This proposed railway was to be narrow gauge and two schemes were under consideration: one was to head for Forrest by Auldgirth station along a similar route to that proposed in the 1860s, and the other was to run through Dunscore and Laggan as far as Portrack on the G&SW main line and from there turn south towards Holywood station. Mr Bruce, another Edinburgh engineer, explained that the cost of the latter route would be about £18,000 less than that of the Auldgirth line. He went on to describe how goods could be transferred between trucks on the standard gauge main line and those on the narrow gauge branch by means of a steam-powered crane, stressing that this method was in common use on many minor railways. The meeting heard testimonies for both routes but

The Moniaive to Auldgirth route promoted between 1870 and 1880.

Scottish Records Office/British Railways Board

decided, no doubt due to Mr Bruce's estimate, that the Dunscore to Holywood line was the most favourable option. It was again decided to approach the G&SW for support.

On 4th November a deputation travelled to Glasgow to discuss the possibility of the G&SW providing for the interchange of traffic between the main line and the proposed Moniaive branch at Holywood. The G&SW Company representatives suggested that it might be more suitable to have a new station at Portrack, rather than lay an extra two miles of rails to Holywood. The deputation was pleased with this proposal to save construction costs, which were intended to be raised from local subscriptions rather than by means of any direct funding from the G&SW. This arrangement suited the company Directors who stated that they would make a favourable report on the scheme to their Board and asked to be kept informed of planning and progress.

General interest in the potential benefits from a railway seems to have increased at this time, for a few days later another group met to discuss the possibility of running a line direct from Dumfries to Moniaive. However, this first scheme for a 'Cairn Valley' railway was not pursued any further.

Practical steps were taken at last in November 1871 when notice was given that application was to be made to Parliament to incorporate the Glencairn Railway Company. Contrary to the decision of the previous year the Glencairn company favoured a standard gauge line following the Auldgirth route. A survey was carried out by John Macrae of Edinburgh and a drawing of the line was prepared. Although this new railway scheme had better support, not everyone was totally convinced of its merits. For example, the Glencairn Free Church minister, Revd Patrick Borrowman, was unhappy at 'the prospect of the iron horse disturbing the peace of the Cairn Valley'. But he consoled himself with the thought that it would be a long time before the railway was built. He also understood that: 'It was to be a very quiet harmless affair and that it would be as like the stage coaches as possible; the trains would not run over fast and they would stop anywhere if you held up your stick or umbrella within sight of the driver'.

Revd Borrowman certainly was correct about the time taken for building; he died in 1899 and never saw a railway to Moniaive.

The Glencairn Railway Bill was passed on 6th August, 1872, but only after long discussions between the promoters and the G&SW as to their involvement in the scheme. The problem was that the promoters now wanted the G&SW not only to undertake to operate the line, but also to subscribe towards its construction. However, the Directors of the G&SW were not prepared to recommend that their shareholders should invest in the railway and the Glencairn company was forced to seek further local support. This was a major setback and it was May 1878 before the *Standard* reported that the Directors of the Glencairn Railway Company had, 'commenced operations for forming this branch line'. Over the next year and a half, further appeals were made to the G&SW for financial backing, but as before these were rejected.

The promoters carried on regardless and in December 1879 managed to persuade two of the G&SW's Directors to join the Board of the Glencairn Railway Company, which in July 1880 issued a Prospectus for construction of the line. This listed the following Directors:

THE GLENCAIRN RAILWAY COMPANY.

Office—ST. ENOCH STATION, GLASGOW.

APPLICATION FOR SHARES.

To the Directors of the Glencairn Railway Company.

GENTLEMEN,

I request you to allot me _____ Shares of £10 each in the above-named Company, and I agree to accept the same or any less number that may be allotted to me, and I authorise you to place my name on the Register of Members of the Company in respect of the Shares so allotted.

I have paid to the Union Bank of
Scotland at _____
Or, I enclose to you
} The sum of £ _____

being a deposit of £1 per Share on the above Shares.

Name in full _____

Address _____

Designation _____

Date _____

Signature _____

THE GLENCAIRN RAILWAY COMPANY.

BANKERS' RECEIPT.

Received this _____ day of _____ 1880, of

Mr. _____ the sum of £ _____

being a deposit of £1 per Share on _____ Shares of £10 each in

the above-named Company.

Signed _____

Application form for shares in the Glencairn Railway Company, 1880.
Dumfries & Galloway Libraries, Information & Archives

Peter Clouston, Chairman of the G&SW
Benjamin Nicholson, Director of the G&SW
James McCall of Caitloch, Moniaive
John McMillan of Holm and Glencrosh, Moniaive
William Smith of Hastings Hall, Moniaive

The railway was to be about 10½ miles long and single track throughout. The Prospectus claimed that the total cost would be £65,000 of which £40,000 already had been pledged. It also stated that: 'The Railway will not only be of great advantage to the proprietors in the district, but it is believed that, taking a moderate estimate of the revenue, a fair return will be obtained for the capital expended; and that, too, immediately on the Line being opened for traffic'.

Despite the apparent plausibility of the Prospectus, the necessary capital could not be raised and in a last-ditch effort, the G&SW was again approached for help. The response was curt, warranting only a short entry in the G&SW Directors' minutes for 14th August, 1880, as follows: 'A letter from Messrs Paterson making a proposal for the carrying out the scheme for making this railway was read out, and the proposal declined'.

In early September 1880 the promoters of the Glencairn branch were forced to issue a circular stating that the project had been abandoned. The Glencairn Railway Company was dissolved formally on 27th June, 1881. It now seems a touch hypocritical of the *Standard*, which had been so enthusiastic about the Auldgirth railway, to conclude that:

It is in some respects a pity that the valley of the Cairn should be left without the obvious advantages which a railway affords, but to many of its sons the failure of the scheme will not be an unmixed disappointment. Their regret will be tempered with the feeling of satisfaction that the home of their childhood is to remain the sequestered spot with which they are familiar, its tranquillity unbroken by the shrill screech of the steam whistle; and even to the casual tourist it is something in these days of rapid and easy travelling to find a village so large and so beautifully situated as Moniaive, which is still comparatively difficult to access.

It was 1896 before another committee issued a petition to promote a line to Moniaive. The proposed route had reverted to that favoured by Mr McCall and his friends over 31 years earlier - from Moniaive through Penpont to Thornhill. But, rather than Moniaive, the impetus for this scheme came from Penpont.

The *Standard* of 30th May reported that the Penpont petition was 'being practically signed *en masse* by the people of the district, and similar forms of petition are being printed for signature in Thornhill and Tynron'. The document stated that the railway could replace road traffic and also open up new trade in the district, particularly stone, lime, milk and feedstuffs. In addition, it was suggested that a new station could be provided to serve Thornhill more conveniently, as the town was a mile from its main line station.

The recipients of the petition were once again the Directors of the G&SW, who were impressed enough to send a survey party to Thornhill in June. The *Standard* noted that after Penpont there were two possible routes to Moniaive: one would follow the natural hill passes, while the other would require deep cuttings in order to carry the line through Tynron village. The *Standard's* reporter also speculated that the railway could connect eventually with Carsphairn, Dalmellington and Ayr. Almost as a footnote, the writer added that several of the prominent landowners in Glencairn Parish had expressed an interest in building a line from Moniaive direct to Dumfries.

However, this alternative scheme for a direct line to Dumfries soon grew in popularity, and in August the Parish Councils of Glencairn, Dunscore and Irongray approached their counterparts on the Town Council of Dumfries to seek further support. The thought of a railway bringing new trade into Dumfries appealed greatly to the town bailies and the Cairn Valley proposal received their unreserved backing. This was the start of a bitter rivalry between the supporters of the two lines.

On 11th September, 1896 several of the Directors of the G&SW travelled to Thornhill to meet a deputation in favour of forming the line from there to Moniaive. Mr Paterson, a local solicitor, described the nature of the expected goods and livestock traffic and also highlighted the tourist potential of the area. He was backed up by several other farmers and businessmen, one threatening darkly that 'if the line were taken down the Cairn Valley, the Caledonian Railway would step in and the G&SW would lose at present what they had all to themselves'. Sir William Renny Watson, the Chairman of the G&SW, thanked the members of the deputation for their attendance, but reminded them that his Board was still free to open a line over either of the proposed routes.

The Cairn Valley Railway's supporters in turn met the Board on 6th October. Mr Maxwell of Munches, who was once a Director of the G&SW, put forward a strong case to his former colleagues at their Glasgow offices. He emphasised that the Cairn Valley line was the most direct route to Dumfries, which was the principal market town in the district, and that on the rival railway, passengers for further afield would have to change at Thornhill and then take a local train before changing again at Dumfries.

A memorandum was then circulated which explained the commercial and engineering advantages of the Dumfries route. This document claimed that the Cairn Valley Railway would: serve a new large area; have few roads and rivers to cross; rise only 320 feet over 16 miles; and have no opposition from the landowners along its route. On the other hand, it contended that the Thornhill line would: serve a smaller district; cross several roads and streams; be as steep as 1 in 33 at one point and run through land which was owned by a non-resident landlord (the Duke of Buccleuch), and farmers who were opposed to its construction.

As with the Thornhill deputation, the company's response was guarded. Sir Renny Watson stated that the Directors were not committed to either scheme, nor indeed to build a line, but their engineer would survey the route of the proposed railway.

The Thornhill committee responded swiftly to the Moniaive memorandum. One of its members wrote to the *Standard* stating that most of the trade from Moniaive was with the North and West and that a line to Thornhill would be the most commercial proposition for the G&SW. The letter continued in scathing tone: 'when one considers for a moment what the Cairn Valley undertaking means to the Glasgow and South-Western Railway Company, one cannot but admire the bland and child-like air of the deputation and the cool audacity of their request'.

More public meetings followed in Thornhill, Penpont and Tynron at which the contents of the Cairn Valley memorandum were hotly disputed. The Thornhill committee then produced its own document and presented it to the G&SW at its November Board meeting. This compared the different schemes and emphasised the merits of their proposed railway in terms of its potential passenger and goods trade. Meanwhile the people of Moniaive were still certain that the line would be run up the Cairn Valley. For example young Fergus Paterson of Kilniess Moniaive wrote confidently to his mother on 17th November, 1896: 'Have you heard that the railway is coming from Dumfries by Dunscore?'

All this acrimony between the two committees did at least create enough public interest to convince the G&SW that some form of Moniaive railway would be viable. The Directors weighed up the options carefully. In terms of engineering works, both lines would be more difficult to construct than claimed by their supporters. Although the Thornhill route was the shorter by several miles, its rival had the backing of Dumfries Town Council and the people of Moniaive, which would be the terminus of either line and therefore the source of most of its trade. The Cairn Valley Railway could possibly be extended west into Galloway and perhaps even provide a direct connection between the towns of Dumfries and Ayr.

On 9th February, 1897 the G&SW held a special shareholders' meeting to explain its decision to construct the Cairn Valley Railway. When asked if the scheme would be profitable, Sir Renny Watson stressed that the Directors would minimise construction costs and that the new line would feed the main rail network to the advantage of the company and its shareholders.

Objections from the Caledonian Railway came to nothing and the Glasgow and South-Western Railway Act of 6th August, 1897 authorised the construction of seven new lines, including the Cairn Valley Railway at an estimated cost of £165,840. The Act described its route as follows:

A railway (No. 6) 15 miles 6 furlongs 2 chains and 14 yards in length commencing in the parish of Holywood in the county of Dumfries by a junction with the Company's Glasgow Dumfries and Carlisle Railway and terminating in the parish of Glencairn in the same county at a point seventy yards or thereabouts measured in a south-easterly direction from Moniaive Public School.

However, the *Standard* of 13th November, 1897 reported that the Directors of the G&SW intended to postpone building the railway until 1899. They hoped to take advantage of the Light Railways Act of 1896, which was passed to encourage rural rail communications by making some engineering and signalling requirements less stringent than on standard lines. On 4th October, 1898 the G&SW Company's solicitors were instructed to make a formal application to the Light Railway Commissioners seeking permission to form the Cairn Valley line as a light railway at an estimated cost of £123,857, including contingency of £9,813.

LIGHT RAILWAYS ACT 1896.

GLASGOW AND SOUTH-WESTERN RAILWAY (CAIRN VALLEY LIGHT RAILWAY) ORDER 1899.

ORDER

MADE BY THE

LIGHT RAILWAY COMMISSIONERS,

AND MODIFIED AND CONFIRMED BY THE

BOARD OF TRADE,

AUTHORISING THE

GLASGOW AND SOUTH-WESTERN RAILWAY COMPANY TO CONSTRUCT AND WORK AS A LIGHT RAILWAY THE CAIRN VALLEY RAILWAY, WHICH THE SAID COMPANY HAVE POWER TO CONSTRUCT AND WORK UNDER THE GLASGOW AND SOUTH-WESTERN RAILWAY ACT, 1897.

Presented to both Houses of Parliament by Command of Her Majesty.

LONDON:
PRINTED FOR HER MAJESTY'S STATIONERY OFFICE,
By DARLING & SON, LTD., 1-3, GREAT ST. THOMAS APOSTLE, E.C.

And to be purchased, either directly or through any Bookseller, from
EYRE & SPOTTISWOODE, EAST HARDING STREET, FLEET STREET, E.C.; and
32, ABINGDON STREET, WESTMINSTER, S.W.; or
JOHN MENZIES & CO., 12, HANOVER STREET, EDINBURGH, and
90, WEST NILE STREET, GLASGOW; or
HODGES, FIGGIS, & CO., LIMITED, 104, GRAFTON STREET, DUBLIN.

1900.

[Cd. 64.]   *Price* 1½*d.*

Title page of the Cairn Valley Light Railway Order of 1899.   *Author's Collection*

On 21st February, 1899 the G&SW held another special shareholders' meeting, this time to describe the reasons for the changes in design of the proposed railway. Mr Charlton of Dumfries asked the Chairman whether the line would be a tramway or a properly constructed railway with bridges and stations and how soon the Directors intended work to start. Sir Renny Watson assured Mr Charlton that the railway would be laid soon, and that it would follow the best possible route through the countryside and not the road, as would a typical tramway. He also explained that the line would serve equally as well as an ordinary branch but would be cheaper to build and operate. Mr Charlton was pleased with the Chairman's response which he thought would allay fears in the Moniaive district that the light railway scheme was an attempt by the company to postpone, or even cancel, the line's construction.

The G&SW intended that the light railway would follow a slightly different route from that authorised in 1897, but the Board of Trade stated that this was not acceptable and the company was forced to revert to its original survey. The Light Railway Commission approved the company's application on 25th April and the *Standard* reported that: 'It is, therefore, virtually assured that in a few months at most the Company will be furnished with an order authorizing them to construct the line, and requiring them to complete and open it for traffic on or before the 6th August, 1902, under a penalty of £50 for every day's delay after that date'.

The Glasgow and South-Western (Cairn Valley Light Railway) Order was confirmed by the Board of Trade on 29th December, 1899. After 35 years of almost continual effort a rail connection to Moniaive was assured at last.

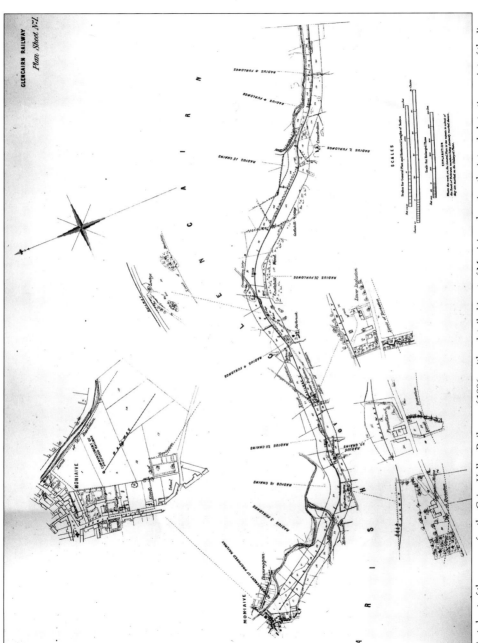

First sheet of the survey for the Cairn Valley Railway of 1896, with a detailed inset of Moniaive, showing the intended starting point of the line.
Scottish Records Office/British Railways Board

Chapter Two

Construction

Good weather in May and June 1901 helped early work on the railway and a temporary line, to allow movement of materials, was soon laid out towards the Dumfries to Holywood road. A great amount of cutting and excavation was necessary in the first six miles and this work was undertaken from the outset. The engineers estimated that over 60,000 yards of material had to be shifted from this section. The work was carried out by gangs of men aided by one engine and nine horses until, at the end of June, two 'steam navvies' were also put into operation, each of which could displace between 500 and 600 yards of material per day. Most of the 200 men hired to build the line were housed in Dumfries to begin with, but as work progressed, Mitchell Brothers, the contractor, erected a number of timber lodging huts along the route of the railway. The first two huts, accommodating 22 men each, were put up at Gateside near Irongray and a hut for 10 men and stables were built nearby at Birkhall.

In August 1901, the ministers of Glencairn, Dunscore, Irongray and Holywood parishes approached the Scottish Navvy Mission and obtained the services of Mr Arthur Scruton to tend to the practical and spiritual welfare of the workmen. No doubt the churchmen were also intending that Mr Scruton would ensure that the morals of the local populace were not corrupted by the hard-living navvies. Mr Scruton, who was engaged for an initial period of four months at a salary of £7 per month, was apparently a popular choice with the navvies. His duties were to give sermons and hold talks, dress any minor wounds and distribute 'wholesome reading, newspapers, periodicals and magazines'. Mr Scruton was pleased with the conditions at the works, stating that in 14 years experience he had never seen such excellent and well arranged huts for navvies. He expressed his satisfaction to the parish ministers in this report:

> I arrived at Dumfries on July 30th, and walked to Morrington, where I have taken a cottage near the works. I began work the first Sabbath in August by conducting four meetings in the huts . A number of the men, I regret to say, were under the influence of strong drink. The rest were very attentive to both the reading and preaching of God's Word, while all were quite respectful. There are five huts erected to lodge 24 men each, and these have been well filled. There is also the manager's hut. Two more huts for navvies are being built at Drumpark, a mile from here. As our house is situated almost in the centre of the huts, I shall be able to work the whole for some time without having to remove.
>
> I have visited the works 16 times and have had six short services or informal talks with the men while they have been at dinner. I have conducted 15 Sabbath meetings in the huts, the numbers attending being good on the whole. As a rule, I leave home at ten am and return again at five pm. The nature of the work varies, and one has something new to do every day. There is preaching the Gospel to all, personal dealing, ambulance work, letter-writing, mending clothes, hair-cutting, &c: in fact anything to help the men, influence them for good, and win them for Christ. Through personal dealing, two

MONIAIVE

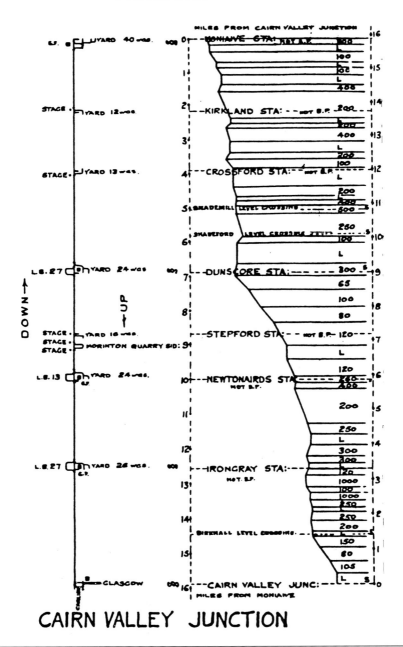

CAIRN VALLEY JUNCTION

Extract from the LMS gradient profiles, showing the distance between stations and the capacity of the yards and sidings at each.

Scottish Records Office/British Railways Board

masons signed the Temperance pledge on the works last week. I try to make every visit and talk as beneficial as possible. During August, 32 men have had something done for them in the way of having wounds, cuts, and sores dressed. Sometimes before we can preach to a man he must be fed and clothed; and this I have often had to do here. The contractors are very kind and desire to see the Mission a success amongst the men on their works. Everything is being done to keep intoxicating drink out of the huts. Two hut-keepers have been turned away already for selling liquor to the men.

Both hut-keepers and men have given me a hearty welcome. A few of them want to live better. I sincerely ask the prayer of all interested in this work. May God add His divine blessing.

> Yours Faithfully,
> ARTHUR SCRUTON
> MORRINTON, August 31st, 1901.

Despite Mr Scruton's belief in the general good character of the mainly Irish navvies, their arrival added a certain colour to the villages of the Cairn Valley. Willie Rankine, a long time resident of Dunscore, wrote this of an incident, which he recalled happening in a cellar below the old King's Arms Hotel:

> The cellar was used as a barber's shop in the years when the navvies were building the Cairn Valley Railway. My blacksmith father was barber in the evenings. One night a big Irish navvy, who had no doubt had one too many in the King's Arms took possession of the razor and threatened the throats of all comers. However, the village policeman took over and advised my father to close down, and so avoid any more 'close shaves'.

The workmen also brought a smallpox scare to the valley. Two nurses were sent to Snade, near Dunscore, to care for the patients and vaccinate the local children and this measure limited the spread of the disease to two or three cases.

The work was more difficult than the contractor had anticipated. For example, the land in the region of the main line junction was extremely spongy and it swallowed over 100,000 tons of material before a firm track bed could be formed. On 6th August, 1902 the time allotted for completion ran out with the railway still unfinished. The G&SW was forced to seek an extension period, which was granted through a Provisional Parliamentary Order, allowing a further two years to complete the work.

A succession of wet seasons did not help matters. The railway followed the route of the Cluden and Cairn waters very closely over most of its length and a heavy flood in 1903 hindered progress by washing away parts of the embankments. Then a good deal of further banking and cutting had to be faced, the most extensive of which was at Dalgonar, near Dunscore station, where unexpectedly difficult excavations to a depth of 40 feet were needed. The original test borings had indicated nothing worse than light gravel, however this covered a tenacious deposit of boulder clay. The contractor claimed against the railway company and after the case was referred to an arbitrator, was awarded £33,483 12s. 10d. plus an additional sum of £2,394 10s. 4d. for the rock cutting.

The workings became easier as they neared Moniaive. The workforce also had grown to around 400 men and consequently construction progressed more

Steam navvy at work on the construction of the railway, taken about 1903.

Christine Hiddleston

quickly. A further extension order was obtained in August 1904, but by then completion was a formality. Indeed, in that month a party of journalists was taken on a run along the railway by special train. Stops were made to allow the resident engineer and the inspector of works to describe the route and the nature of the civil engineering undertaken. The train was hauled by one of the contractor's small engines and some of the party elected to travel in an open-topped seated truck in order to get a better view of the scenery and points of interest. The *Dumfries and Galloway Standard* reported that a large number of men at Dalgonar were still engaged in finishing the sides of the deep cutting and laying the permanent way. Temporary rails were in use there and near Moniaive, where some final levelling, banking and building were also being undertaken.

The completed railway had four principal stations: Irongray, Newtonairds, Dunscore and Moniaive. The original specification called for a station at Drumpark, which is very close to Newtonairds but on the other side of the Cairn. However, this requirement was removed and Newtonairds station was located to serve both places with a new road bridge providing access from Drumpark to the station. Each station building cost £212 to build and comprised of a booking office and waiting room, constructed in red brick with cream-painted poster boards and chocolate-coloured framing. An extension was fitted over the front and this and the main roof were covered with red tiles. Yards and sidings were laid out to cater for goods traffic and crossing loops were provided. Moniaive station was the largest, with a passenger platform nearly 90 yards long and a line of rails laid along both sides. There was a large goods shed and adjoining it a loading bank for live stock. Another set of rails, which ended at the loading bank, served as a shunting lye. An engine shed was put up at the foot of the village, opposite the present football park. A turntable was costed in the list of equipment for the line, but if this was ever fitted at Moniaive, it was never used in earnest as the engine always ran backwards to Dumfries. The other main stations had no large sheds, but Dunscore had a notable feature in the water columns and tanks fitted at each end of the station platform.

Three other minor stations - Crossford, Kirkland and Stepford - were designated as stopping places and provided with little more than a tin shelter for passengers and a short siding with a loading bank to enable goods to be handled. The G&SW spent much less on the construction of these halts, for example the passenger shelters cost only £13 each, however, the company offered prizes to encourage its staff to lay out flower beds and make each station as pretty as possible.

Houses were provided for station masters and crossing keepers. Some of these, for example Kirkland, Crossford, Snademill and Snadeford, were built to a standard company pattern with a pyramid roof truncated by a central chimney stack, while others, such as Stepford and Moniaive, were traditional-style cottages.

The standard-gauge track was single throughout and laid in accordance with the Light Railway Order using rails of at least 70 lb. per yard. These had to be attached to the sleepers by fang bolts or coach screws at the ends and double spikes and bearing plates along their length.

An early postcard view of Newtonairds station taken by J. Laurie of Dunscore. The station buildings were similar at Irongray, Dunscore and Moniaive.   *Malcolm Chadwick Collection*

Another postcard from the same series, this time showing the basic passenger facilities at Stepford station.   *Author's Collection*

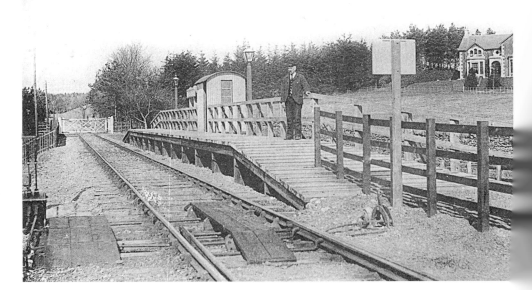

The line started off fairly straight and level, passing to the east of the signal box at Cairn Valley Junction. The Cluden was crossed near Irongray by means of a 130 ft-long iron-girdered viaduct supported by six stone piers. A second bridge carried the line over the Auld Water of Cluden, a tributary of the Cairn, which was also crossed just below Newtonairds. The railway began to climb uphill as it ran hard by the side of the river towards Stepford. The gradients in the next section were severe, increasing from 1 in 80 to 1 in 65 just below Dunscore station where a brick-faced viaduct of three arches spanned the Cairn. The railway then snaked its way up through Crossford and Kirkland, twisting and turning along the riverbank before straightening out into the terminus at Moniaive. The Cairn was crossed for the last time in this section at Gaupsmill farm, and finally, the Dalwhat water was bridged near the bottom of the village.

The main stations were provided with home and starting banner signals for both directions. These were controlled electrically; the only other fixed signals were ground discs at Cairn Valley Junction, Irongray and Moniaive for passing into sidings and loop lines. The sidings at each stopping place were fitted with ground frames controlled by an Annett's key which was kept in a locked box to prevent misuse. A telephone system was installed to provide communications between each station on the line, Dumfries Telegraph Office and Lockerbie Junction signal box.

The railway had six level crossings, one each at Irongray, Stepford and Crossford, and the others at points where the line passed over minor roadways. The Light Railway Order required the crossings to be fitted with gates, although some of these hardly seemed necessary. For example, the road at Snademill was only a short gravel track running down to the river. Each gatehouse was fitted with warning bells to announce that a train was approaching and a disc indicator to show its direction. The total construction costs for the completed railway (excluding permanent way materials which were supplied 'free issue' by the G&SW) were as shown below:

Item	Cost		
	£	s.	d.
Civil Engineering Tender	82,279	16	6
Arbitration Settlement	33,483	12	10
Additional Rock Cutting	2,394	10	4
Station Buildings	887	0	0
Station Houses	3,270	0	0
Goods and Engine Sheds, Water Tanks, Weighing Machines, Gates and Lamps, Signalling at Cairn Valley Junction and Turntable	2,424	0	0
Sykes' Electric Signalling System	3,133	0	0
Telegraph Wiring	217	5	9
Additional Telegraph Poles	530	0	0
Contractor's Maintenance Fee	600	0	0
Total Cost	129,219	5	5

The people of Moniaive held a meeting in the Public Hall on 19th December, 1904, to consider how best to mark the opening of the railway. The Parish Council had already approached the G&SW to offer hospitality to the railway officials. The manager of the company, Mr David Cooper, had replied that, if it would suit

The three-span viaduct across the Cairn water just below Dunscore station.

R. Maxwell Collection

A contractor's engine on Dunscore viaduct *circa* 1903.   *Christine Hiddleston*

Dunscore station from the west. *Malcolm Chadwick Collection*

Moniaive from the West showing the goods shed to the right. The station had not yet been officially opened when this picture was taken early in 1905. *Author's Collection*

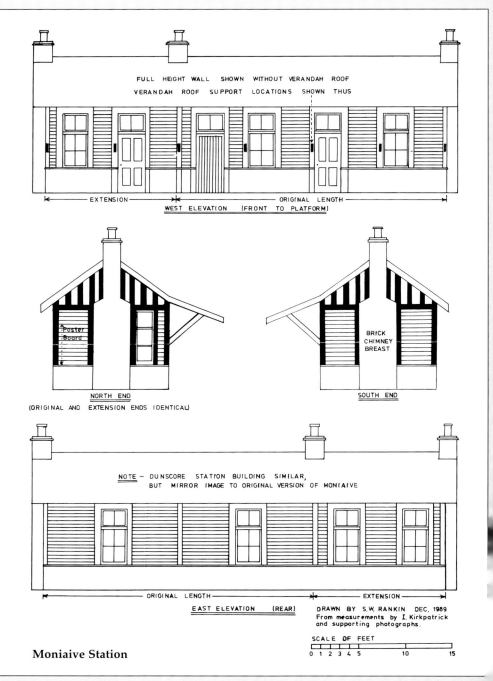

FULL HEIGHT WALL SHOWN WITHOUT VERANDAH ROOF

VERANDAH ROOF SUPPORT LOCATIONS SHOWN THUS

EXTENSION | ORIGINAL LENGTH

WEST ELEVATION (FRONT TO PLATFORM)

Poster Board

NORTH END
(ORIGINAL AND EXTENSION ENDS IDENTICAL)

BRICK CHIMNEY BREAST

SOUTH END

NOTE – DUNSCORE STATION BUILDING SIMILAR, BUT MIRROR IMAGE TO ORIGINAL VERSION OF MONIAIVE

ORIGINAL LENGTH | EXTENSION

EAST ELEVATION (REAR)

DRAWN BY S.W. RANKIN DEC. 1989
From measurements by I. Kirkpatrick and supporting photographs.

SCALE OF FEET
0 1 2 3 4 5   10   15

Moniaive Station

Drawings of Moniaive station building prepared from measurements taken in 1989. The extension on the north side of the building provided a separate station master's office.

S.W. Rankin/G&SW Railway Association

local parties, the official opening should be held on the 31st December, when a deputation of the chief officials would be glad to attend any function arranged for them at Moniaive. All the guests were also given the opportunity to have a run along the line to Dumfries and back. After some discussion it was agreed to accept Mr Cooper's proposals and that a public luncheon should be held in the village on the 31st followed by a Grand Ball on the 2nd January. Four days later these plans had to be changed as the Board of Trade examination to approve the line's fitness for service could not be performed in time. The opening ceremony had to be postponed, but as a consolation the Ball went ahead as planned.

The committee appointed to organize the opening celebrations next heard from Mr Cooper in February. The G&SW intended to open the railway for normal traffic on 1st March, 1905, subject to the consent of the Board of Trade. They also proposed that the official opening should take place on 28th February. The committee approved these arrangements with satisfaction.

The signalling system for the Cairn Valley line was examined by Major J.W. Pringle of the Board of Trade, who could not authorise the Sykes' system as secure enough for operations, and reported that a Train Staff and Ticket system should be used until his recommendations were implemented and the Sykes' interlocking was fully tested. With only 12 days to go until the line opened it was impractical for the G&SW to get the necessary modifications done in time and the Train Staff and Ticket system proposal must have been a welcome compromise to allow services to begin. Major Pringle described the required changes to the Sykes' system in his report of 16th February, 1905:

Cairn Valley Junction - No. 7 points to be made for the Branch Line and to be locked in that position by the point lock operated by No. 7. [This was necessary to allow a down branch train to be accepted as far as the down electric starting signal whilst an up branch train was approaching the up (electric) outer home. But this method of working was only allowable when the up branch was a passenger train. Nos. 6 and 7 would then be required to hold 16.]

Irongray - The Cairn Valley block instrument to lock with Nos. 4 and 6 point locks and to lock No. 2 points both ways. The Newtonairds block instrument to lock Nos. 3 and 5 points both ways. A new up starting to be provided in advance of the the loop points and was to act as the block controlling signal. The existing starting signal to be operated by a switch from the signal box and to be controlled as it then was by the level crossing gates.

Newtonairds - The Irongray block instrument to lock with 4 and 6 point locks and to lock No. 2 points both ways. The Dunscore block instrument to interlock with No. 1 points lock and to lock 3 and 5 both ways.

Dunscore - The Moniaive block instrument to interlock with No. 1 point lock and to lock 3 and 5 both ways. The Newtonairds instrument to interlock with No. 4 and 6 points and to lock 2 points both ways.

Moniaive Station - The Dunscore block instrument to lock No. 3 points both ways.

On 20th February, a special train flitted the station masters, their families and household furniture to their respective stations. The agents appointed were as follows: Moniaive, Mr Wilkie, Abercorn; Kirkland, Mr Holmes, who was a porter at Cassillis and was to be under the Moniaive agent; Crossford, Mr Telfer, formerly porter at Paisley West; Dunscore, Mr Drummond, Hawkhead, who was to control Crossford and Stepford; Stepford, Mr Irving, porter from Auldgirth;

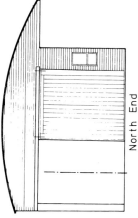

North End

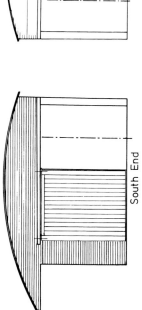

South End

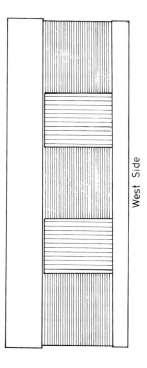

West Side

Moniaive goods shed. The building still exists but is much altered from the original condition shown here.
S.W. Rankin/G&SW Railway Association

MONIAIVE GOODS SHED

CORRUGATED IRON WALLS & ROOF.
(BRICK BASE,

Drawn by S.W. Rankin December 1990
Based on measurements by I. Kirkpatrick and photographs

Scale of Feet

| 0 | 5 | 10 | 15 | 20 | 25 |

Moniaive Station

An early postcard by J. Laurie of the station and staff at Moniaive. *Author's Collection*

Newtonairds, Mr Nicholson, clerk from Auldgirth; Irongray, Mr Barr, Rigg. The station master at Stepford was to have been Mr David Beattie, a signalman at Dumfries, however a terrible accident made this appointment impossible.

Mr Beattie and another signalman were walking home one evening and for a short cut they decided to go along the six-foot way between the up and down rails. The engine of a passenger train uncoupled to shunt a van into the yard and came along van first, tender next and engine last so that the driver's view was obstructed. Mr Beattie was watching the signal in front and seeing that it was at danger he thought he was safe. The engine driver saw that the signal was against him but decided to draw up close to it. The train ran up so quietly that Mr Beattie never heard its approach and he was caught and knocked down by the foot board of the van. He fell across the rails and the train ran over his legs, almost severing them. Doctors arrived quickly but they were unable to save his legs, which had to be amputated above the knees. Mr Beattie faced a long spell in Dumfries infirmary and had little chance of future employment. However, he was a resilient character and when the railway finally came to Moniaive, he sent some lines celebrating the event to the *Standard*. His merits as a poet are debatable, but his sentiments were definitely in the right place, as the first and last verses show:

> *Hip, hip hurrah it's through at last*
> *We'd unco lang tae wait;*
> *But noo we've got a rich reward,*
> *That pays for being late.*

> *In fact, alang the glen ye'll fin',*
> *That every ane will thrive,*
> *Noo that the line is opened,*
> *Frae Dumfries tae Moniaive.*

Glasgow and South-Western Railway

GENERAL MANAGER'S OFFICE,
St. Enoch Station,
GLASGOW, 23rd February, 1905.

CIRCULAR No. 955.

Dear Sir,

CAIRN VALLEY LIGHT RAILWAY.

The above Railway will be opened on Wednesday, 1st March, for the conveyance of Passengers and Merchandise Traffic.

The following are the names of the Stations, with the accommodation provided thereat :—

								Crane Power.	
								T.	C.
Irongray,	-	-	-	G	P	F	L	H	C	—
Newtonairds,	-	-	G	P	F	L	H	C	—
Stepford,	-	-	G	P	—	L	H	—	—
Dunscore,	-	-	G	P	F	L	H	C	—
Crossford,	-	-	G	P	—	L	H	—	—
Kirkland,	-	-	G	P	—	L	H	—	—
Moniaive,	-	-	G	P	F	L	H	C	1 10

The following appointments have been made :—

Mr. JAMES BARR, - - Agent, Irongray.
Mr. WILLIAM NICHOLSON, Agent, Newtonairds.
Mr. R. M. DRUMMOND, - Agent at Dunscore, with charge also of Stepford and Crossford Depots.
Mr. ARCH. WILKIE, - Agent at Moniaive, with charge also of Kirkland Depot.

All information regarding Rates and Fares and Train Service can be obtained from the Goods Manager or Superintendent of the Line.

DAVID COOPER,
General Manager.

Mr...

....

EXPLANATION.

G—Goods Station.   P—Passenger and Parcel Station.
F—Furniture Vans, Carriages, Portable Engines, and Machines on Wheels.
L—Live Stock.   H—Horse Boxes and Prize Cattle Vans.   C—Carriages by Passenger Train.

G&SW circular advising of the opening of the Cairn Valley Light Railway.
Scottish Records Office/British Railways Board

Chapter Three

Opening Day

The weather on the morning of 28th February was wet and cold and the hills surrounding Moniaive were still capped with snow that had fallen the previous day. The village streets were empty and the only outward signs that the railway was finally about to arrive in Moniaive were the sodden flags which drooped from the shops, houses and the station buildings. However, as the time for the opening ceremony grew nearer a large crowd began to gather at the station. This included the village school children who were let out to witness the special train steam into Moniaive at half past ten.

The train of six corridor coaches was hauled by Manson 4-4-0 No. 190 of '8' class which was highly polished and bedecked with Union Jacks and pennants in the G&SW colours of red and green. It was the final moment of glory for an engine which had once worked the prestigious St Enoch to St Pancras dining-car service but had been relegated latterly to more mundane work at Dumfries. The train was under the care of William McConnell, driver; William Eskdale, fireman; and Kenneth Rae, guard, who were to be permanently employed on the branch. Inspector Dodger of Dumfries was in charge. The passengers from Dumfries included: Mr Charles Cockburn, G&SW line superintendent; Mr Lamb, works resident engineer and Mr Sykes, signalling engineer.

Pictures of the engine, its crew and the assembled crowd were taken by a Dumfries photographer. The engine was then shunted to the back of the train and the Moniaive guests took their seats. These were mainly reserved for landowners and businessmen; however, places were kept for two of the oldest residents of the district, Mr William McGauchie of Dalwhat and retired shoemaker, Mr James McNaught. The ordinary folk who were not invited to travel had to make do with sending celebratory messages by telegram. The train pulled out of the station at 11 o'clock, accompanied by the explosion of fogsignals. A heavy shower fell at the same time but, according to the *Dumfries Courier & Herald* reporter who covered the event, 'this in no way damped the now obvious enthusiasm of the guests and onlookers', who cheered the train's departure.

As the train neared Kirkland station, the passengers saw the Moniaive to Thornhill coach stop on the hillside so that its driver could measure the performance of its new steam-powered rival. More guests joined the train there and at the other intermediate stations which were all decorated with bunting and had fogsignals fitted on the rails for the occasion. The rain stopped and the sun broke through the clouds as the train left the countryside behind and rolled into Dumfries station exactly one hour after leaving Moniaive.

The return journey was scheduled to begin at half past twelve. The train was run into the main northbound line shortly before then and the Dumfries guests took their seats. A fair sized crowd had gathered at Dumfries to witness the proceedings, but as the train set off for Moniaive the *Courier* noted that 'there was little display of enthusiasm'.

An official postcard published by the G&SW Company in 1904 as a precursor to the opening of the Cairn Valley line.   *Author's Collection*

Moniaive from the East, a small place to warrant its own branch line. The station yard can just be made out on the left of the picture.   *Author's Collection*

The first stop was made at Irongray where a party of G&SW representatives joined the train. These included Mr William Melville, the company Engineer and Mr James Manson, the locomotive superintendent. A special train, consisting of an engine and saloon carriage had brought these guests from Glasgow to await the train from Dumfries. The G&SW representatives' special was run on to Moniaive first in order that the return journey to Glasgow could be made directly. The guests' train followed on behind, making more stops at the intermediate stations amid further explosions of fogsignals. The country people were less reserved, and perhaps more impressed by the railway than their counterparts in Dumfries, and the train was cheered by flag-waving onlookers at almost every accessible place along the track.

The following extracts from a contemporary G&SW tourist guide give some flavour of the attractions of the countryside which the guests passed through as they made their way back up the line that day:

Rich in the natural beauties of well-stocked woodlands, moss-covered hills, and fast-flowing crystal streams, 'The Cairn Valley Light Railway', which the enterprise of the Glasgow and South-Western railway has opened up, possesses an absorbing interest. Here it was that some of the most stirring scenes of the Covenanting times were enacted. The birth-place of 'Annie Laurie'; the place where the prototype of 'Jeanie Deans' (Helen Walker), lived and died and is buried, where Carlyle and his wife lived for some six years, and where he wrote the immortal 'Sartor Resartus' ; the hallowed memories of 'Cairn Valley' appeal to every Scotchman. Associated with the history of the 'Valley' are the two great giants of Scottish literature - Sir Walter Scott and Robert Burns. A particularly fine description of the Valley is to be found in the Rev. Dr Walter C. Smith's poem of 'Boreland Hall', and that gem of pastoral love songs, 'Ca' the Ewes tae the Knowes', is inseparably associated with this delightful valley.

Leaving Dumfries, the main line is traversed for some two miles, when Lincluden Abbey is seen on the left, just as the train passes the last of the Dumfries Villas, and a little further on this branch leaves the main line near Holywood. As already mentioned the first station is Irongray. Here in the the graveyard adjoining the Parish Church lies Helen Walker, whose unblemished character and heroic self-sacrifice are immortalized in the 'Heart of Midlothian'. Over her grave is a flat or 'table' tombstone placed there by Sir Walter Scott, and bearing an epitaph written by him. For the next two miles, till Newtonairds is reached the line runs along the Cluden, which a little to the south of Newtonairds, is joined by the Cairn Water - a good fishing stream. We notice two mansion houses here, Drumpark on the left and Newtonairds on the right. 'Boreland Hall', which gave the title to Dr Walter C. Smith's poem, lies at the foot of Sceoch Hill, a little to the south-east of Drumpark. The 'Routen Brig',with its picturesque little waterfall, in the immediate vicinity of Newtonairds, is a favourite spot with picnic parties.

The next station is Stepford, nestling at the foot of Killyleoch Hill, the village presenting a neat and clean appearance. Before reaching Dunscore, a little over two miles further on, a good view of Dunscore Kirk is to be had. The village of Dunscore is remarkable in its general cleanliness and tidiness. It is 400 feet above sea level ; the air is bracing and invigorating, and as a health resort it is much in demand. About a mile to the north-east is 'Lag Tower', the scene of 'Wanderin' Willie's' tale in 'Redgauntlet'. 'Lag Tower' built in the time of James III, was the stronghold of Sir Robert Grierson, whose persecution of the Covenanters, their wives and families, is one of the saddest chapters in Scottish history.

Between Dunscore and Moniaive are the stations of Crossford and Kirkland. To the west of Crossford is Maxwelton House, the seat of the Rev. Sir Emilius Laurie, Bart, and anciently the castle of the Earls of Glencairn. Here was born in 1682, 'Bonnie Annie Laurie', the heroine of the well known song. The original ballad of 'Maxwelton Braes'

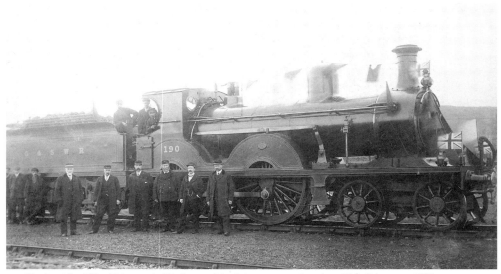

Engine No. 190 of Manson's '8' class at Moniaive on opening day, 28th February, 1905.
Glasgow & South Western Railway Association

Crowd at Moniaive assembled in front of the first train.
Dumfries & Galloway Libraries, Information & Archives

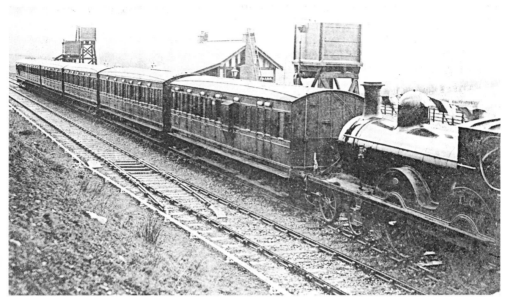

The first train from Moniaive, at Dunscore station, 28th February, 1905. *Author's Collection*

A selection of tickets from the first day of operation of the railway. *Brian Hilton*

was the composition of the lady's suitor, Douglas of Fingland. The modern version, now universally sung, is by Lady John Scott, a member of the Spottiswood family, and sister-in-law of the late Duke of Buccleuch. 'Annie Laurie', a portrait of whom still hangs in Maxwelton House, lived to the age of 82, and is buried in Glencairn Churchyard. Near to Kirkland Station are the mansion houses of Crawfordton and Jarbruck. On the Jarbruck Estate is an ancient moat, which figures in local legends as the 'Bow-Butts of Ingleston', archery having been at one time practised on its borders. The moat is quite close to the railway, and consists of a long bank with a mound at each end.

Moniaive, the termination of the line, is a place of some antiquity. It was created a Burgh of Barony by Royal Charter in the reign of Charles I. In 1638, to commemorate the 'Charter of Charles', a stone pillar in the shape of an ancient cross, 14 feet high, was erected in the centre of the village. On an eminence in the west-end of the village stands a monument, erected by public subscription in 1828, to the memory of the Rev. James Renwick, the last person who suffered death in Scotland as a Covenanter.

The train reached Moniaive station about 1.20 pm where the dignitaries were delighted to see a long line of children bearing welcoming banners. A luncheon for the local committee and their guests was held in the Public Hall at two o'clock. Around 130 people were present. The *Dumfries and Galloway Standard* reported that, 'the recherche' luncheon, purveyed by Mrs Oliver of the Craigdarroch Arms Hotel' was 'very smartly served'.

During lunch, Revd Patrick Playfair, a former Minister of the Parish, traced the history of the various proposals for a Glencairn railway over the previous 40 years and acknowledged with pleasure the presence of Mr William Kennedy of Townhead, Glencairn, who had been involved in the very first scheme to run a line from Moniaive to Penpont and Thornhill. Revd Playfair made much of the tourist potential of the district which the railway would make more readily accessible. He also emphasised the importance of the line connecting with Dumfries directly, rather than via Thornhill as had been proposed, stating that:

> Time is of value, and transit of stock and goods must be as speedy as possible. We want all the facilities which we can have in our own country, railway and other, to help us to meet the increasing competition which oppresses us from other lands. And a railway company which helps in opening up such a district as this is in very truth acting in a most patriotic manner and is carrying out a most benevolent role in the story of the nations.

Provost Glover of Dumfries proposed the toast to the contractors, pointing out that Messrs Mitchell 'had opened up a district typical of the finest manhood in the kingdom'. In reply, Mr Mitchell was good enough to mention Mr Glover's forthcoming Parliamentary candidature. More toasts followed and the proceedings ended with the National Anthem. The G&SW party left for Glasgow about four o'clock and as soon as their train had reached Dunscore the other train set out for Dumfries.

The final word on the coming of the railway goes to the late Bob Hiddleston, who was a blacksmith in Moniaive for many years. When Bob was well into his eighties, he was interviewed on radio where he had a somewhat different recollection of the event's significance:

> A general holiday all round.
> The pubs did well - it was never a temperate place!

Chapter Four

Working the Line

After the excitement of the opening day, it remained to be seen whether the railway would pay as its novelty began to wear off. The line ran through an agricultural district and most weekday passengers were expected to be businessmen and farmers with extra trade on Saturdays from villagers travelling to Dumfries for shopping or entertainment. However, the press and the G&SW had emphasised the scenic and historical attractions of the Cairn Valley and there were high hopes in Moniaive that the railway would help the tourist trade expand, bringing fresh prosperity to the village. John Corrie, the Moniaive postmaster, was one of the optimists. In his *Annals of Glencairn* he wrote:

Many, we know, anticipate the time when Moniaive will become a favourite health resort, and we see no reason why the anticipation should not be realised. During recent years dwellers in our towns and cities have been turning their thoughts more and more towards homes and holiday abodes in the country. To all such, Moniaive offers many attractions. It possesses pure air, beautiful scenery, and peaceful surroundings in abundance.

He also recorded that one delighted passenger had been heard to declare that it was 'well worth travelling up the Cairn Valley line were it only to see the home of bonnie Annie Laurie and the dew-clad braes'.

As well as its fine scenery, the area had sporting appeal; for example a company Tourist Guide listed the Cairn as a good trout and salmon stream. The G&SW was well known as a golfer's railway and soon after the branch was completed Moniaive opened a course, which the same guide described as:

A nine hole course situated on Crichan farm about a quarter of a mile from Moniaive station. The ground is gently sloping and commands magnificent views of the valley of the Cairn. Owing to the nature of the ground the course is rather a sporting one. The holes vary from about 130 to about 150 yards and there are some interesting hazards.

Passenger services, which began on 1st March, 1905, were third class only. There were three trains daily in each direction during the week with extra services on Wednesday, which was market day, and Saturday. The first train left Moniaive at seven o'clock in the morning and the last ran from Dumfries at half past five in the evening, except on Saturdays when an extra service left at ten to nine. Although it took an hour to cover the 17½ miles between Moniaive and Dumfries, this was much quicker than the two to three hours taken by horse and carriage. The fare was also reasonable at 2*s*. 6*d*. return, as the cost by road was about 5*s*. one way when a Light Railway was first proposed in 1897. Other return fares from Dumfries were as follows: Kirkland, 2*s*. 1*d*.; Crossford, 1*s*. 11*d*.; Dunscore, 1*s*. 6*d*.; Stepford, 1*s*. 3*d*.; Newtonairds, 1*s*. 1*d*.; Irongray, 9*d*.

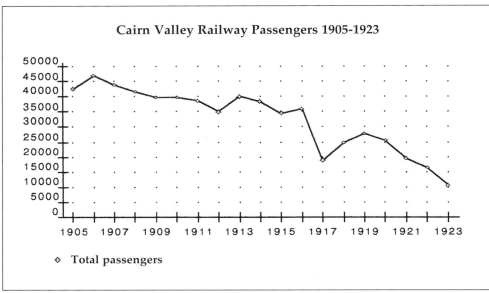

Cairn Valley Railway Passengers 1905-1923

◇ **Total passengers**

Passenger numbers per year over the G&SW period. The trend is obviously downhill for the railway.   *Complied by the author from Scottish Records Office data*

Timber ready for transfer onto the railway in Moniaive station yard.   *Author's Collection*

Cairn Valley Railway Timetable March 1905

Moniaive-Dumfries

		WO	WX	WSO		SO
	am	am	am	pm	pm	pm
Moniaive	7.00	9.55	10.40	1.35	4.00	7.00
Kirkland	7.08	10.03	10.48	1.43	4.08	7.08
Crossford	7.15	10.10	10.55	1.50	4.15	7.15
Dunscore	7.25	10.20	11.05	2.00	4.25	7.25
Stepford	7.30	10.25	11.10	2.05	4.30	7.30
Newtonairds	7.35	10.30	11.15	2.10	4.35	7.35
Irongray	7.45	10.40	11.25	2.20	4.45	7.45
Dumfries	8.00	10.55	11.40	2.35	5.00	8.00

Dumfries-Moniaive

			WSO		SO
	am	pm	pm	pm	pm
Dumfries	8.35	12.15	2.48	5.30	8.50
Irongray	8.50	12.30	3.03	5.45	9.05
Newtonairds	9.00	12.40	3.13	5.55	9.15
Stepford	9.05	12.45	3.18	6.00	9.20
Dunscore	9.10	12.50	3.23	6.05	9.25
Crossford	9.20	1.00	3.33	6.15	9.35
Kirkland	9.27	1.07	3.40	6.22	9.42
Moniaive	9.35	1.15	3.48	6.30	9.50

WO - Wednesday only, WX - Except Wednesday, SO - Saturday only,
WSO - Wednesday & Saturday only

Travellers on the Cairn Valley line were well attended to, with staff at every minor stopping place and crossing. The maximum eight hour day was 13 years away when the line opened and the station masters and crossing keepers were on duty from early morning to mid-evening. Saturday was an especially long day and Sunday must have come as a welcome relief. The working hours are summarised below:

Working Hours at Signal Cabins and Crossings

		On	Off	Sat. Off
		am	pm	pm
Dumfries Cairn Valley Junction			Night and Day	
Irongray	Birkhall	6.30	6.00	9.05
Irongray	Station	6.30	6.00	9.15
Newtonairds	Station	6.40	6.10	9.30
Stepford	Level Crossing	6.45	6.20	9.30
Dunscore	Station	6.45	6.35	10.10
Dunscore	Snadeford	6.45	6.35	9.40
Dunscore	Snademill	6.45	6.35	9.40
Crossford	Level Crossing	6.45	6.35	9.40
Kirkland	Station	6.45	6.30	9.50
Moniaive	Station	6.30	6.40	10.10

The line was operated by means of a development of Sykes' Lock-and-Block signalling system, which was unique at the time for a lengthy single line. This ensured that only one train could enter or leave a section of the railway at any time and then only from a platform line and not a siding. Basically, the system operated in the following manner: when the slider of the block instrument controlling the starting signal was pulled out, it was back-locked electrically so that it could not be replaced until the train had passed over a treadle on the track at the next station and the signalman there had sent the train on down the line. A special switch also was provided to allow the signalman to set a signal to danger before the train had reached the treadle.

There were two main exceptions to ordinary block working. The rear home signal at Cairn Valley Junction could not be lowered unless the points were set to run the train directly into the main line, and the signal at the south end of Irongray station could not be lowered until the crossing-gates were closed across the road. Trains for Moniaive generally passed slowly through Cairn Valley Junction without stopping, but on the return journey there could be a considerable delay as the main northbound line had to be crossed.

The Board of Trade recommended that a Train Staff and Ticket system should be used until the Skyes' signals were tested fully, and as a back up in case of any future faults. This was organised as follows:

Train Staff Section	Colour of Train Staff and Tickets
Cairn Valley Junction to Irongray	Red
Irongray to Newtonairds	Green
Newtonairds to Dunscore	White
Dunscore to Moniaive	Red

The sidings at the stopping places were worked by down trains to Moniaive only. Traffic for Dumfries was taken to the main station in advance and collected on the return journey. When the train had finished shunting, the guard had to make sure that the Annett's key which worked the points was locked away safely in its box and that the box key was delivered to the next main station. From here it was returned eventually to the appropriate signalman in the rear, making it available for collection by the next goods train from Dumfries.

In addition to its novel signalling system, the line was worked by a fairly new type of rolling stock - a combined steam motor and carriage. The engine had outside cylinders, placed between the overall frames and had a carriage directly attached to its rear. The carriage was divided into three compartments, two accommodating up to 50 passengers and the rearmost for the guard. Seats of rattan cane were set lengthways along the sides of the passenger compartments which were lit by Pinscht's oil gas. Hand and vacuum brake controls were fitted in both the cab and the guard's compartment at the rear. The guard also operated a set of retractable steps which could be lowered to let passengers enter from road level. The G&SW usually painted its engines green but the 'railmotor' was finished in crimson lake.

Railmotor No. 1 was designed for the Cairn Valley Railway by the G&SW's locomotive superintendent, James Manson, and was completed at Kilmarnock in September 1904. It was sent to work the Mauchline to Catrine branch until the Moniaive branch was ready for passenger traffic.

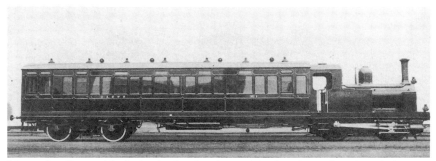

Manson's railmotor No. 1, clearly showing the combined engine and carriage design.
Author's Collection

The railmotor ran engine-first when leaving Dumfries and ran backwards with the motor carriage leading when leaving Moniaive. Two four- or six-wheeled trailers could be attached to the rear of the motor carriage. When running backwards with extra trailers, the fireman rode at the back of the motor carriage and controlled the brake, while the guard kept a look out ahead from the end of the last trailer. When no trailers were attached the guard replaced the fireman in the brake compartment and communicated with the driver by means of an electric bell system.

Two more railmotors were delivered from Kilmarnock in November 1905. On 1st December No. 1 started up a service between Ardrossan and Kilwinning and No. 3 was sent to Moniaive. The railmotor ran smoothly on straight sections, but on tight bends the outside cylinders tended to set up shuddering motions which were transmitted through the engine directly into the carriage. This made the passengers' journey extremely uncomfortable on the upper stretches of the Cairn Valley. Under public pressure, No. 3 was taken out of the frames and given side tanks and a bunker. The engine also was re-painted with G&SW coaching green.

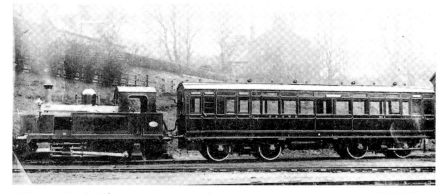

Railmotor No. 3 with separate engine and carriage units.   *J.F. McEwan*

Bryden's coach at Moniaive. The horse-drawn bus ran from Moniaive to Thornhill for over 40 years until the advent of the railway.   *Jock Black*

The less than satisfactory Milnes-Daimler motor-bus that the G&SW operated from 1906 until 1907 as a successor to Bryden's coach.   *Jock Black*

Despite these difficulties the branch was busy when it first opened. The total number of passengers carried in the first 10 months of operation of 1905 was 42,417, which generated an income of £2,265 11s. 10d.

In September 1905 the Board of the G&SW met to discuss the increasing competition from the rapidly expanding Scottish motor-bus services. The Board agreed to run buses of its own through areas which could bring new trade to the company's stations. One of the proposed routes was from Moniaive to Thornhill, which must have been a small consolation to the people of Tynron and Penpont who in 1896 had campaigned for a railway through their villages. In the face of this motorised opposition the horse-drawn bus, which had run twice daily from Moniaive to Thornhill since the 1860s, made its last trip on 30th September, 1905.

The new motor-bus was a single-deck 20 hp Milnes-Daimler which seated 21 passengers. The passenger saloon was entered from a door at the rear and beside this was a ladder which led up to a luggage rack on the roof. The driver's cab was completely open at the sides and front. The only cover was provided by a canopy extension to the roof.

On 5th June, 1906, several of the Directors travelled to Thornhill for a trial run in the bus which made its first official run on 4th July. There were three round trips daily and the fare was 1s. between stations. The company hoped to attract northbound passengers who lived in the Cairn Valley by matching the bus timetable with those of the trains on the main line and the Moniaive branch. However, the bus was slow and often late. Breakdowns also occurred frequently and a horse and carriage had to take over while the bus was under repair. Passengers could not rely on making their connections at Thornhill and preferred instead to take the train to Dumfries before travelling north. The company persevered until the end of October 1907 when the service was withdrawn for good.

Another view of the motor-bus, this time taken in the station yard at Moniaive.
Author's Collection

Stepford station about 1910. The station house can be seen on the left of the picture.

Malcolm Chadwick Collection

There were two goods trains per day, the first from Dumfries at 10.45 am and the second from Moniaive at 1.50 pm. The goods timetable was as follows:

Down			Up		
Dumfries	10.45	*am*	Moniaive	1.50	*pm*
Irongray	11.27		Kirkland	2.02	
Newtonairds	11.42		Crossford	2.10	
Stepford	11.50		Dunscore	2.30	
Dunscore	12.15	*pm*	Stepford	2.40	
Crossford	12.30		Newtonairds	3.15	
Kirkland	12.45		Irongray	3.40	
Moniaive	12.55		Dumfries	4.00	

The 10.45 am goods and 10.40 (Moniaive) passenger trains crossed at Irongray and the 2.48 pm passenger from Dumfries and the 1.50 pm goods passed at Newtonairds.

No. 206A, a rebuilt Stirling '187' class 0-4-2T, was spare at Dumfries for goods work on the branch until withdrawal in 1908. The mainstay of traffic was livestock, timber from Craigdarroch Estate, Moniaive, and road metals from Morrinton quarry, near Stepford. The Moniaive hand laundry was also a customer, taking washing from the many country houses along the line. Mail was carried to and from Dumfries almost immediately after the line opened. By 1909, trade had increased to such an extent that the shunting lyes at the north end of Moniaive station had to be expanded.

The revenue from transport of road metals became increasingly important after 1910 when an aerial ropeway was installed from the rock face at Morrinton quarry, down to a special siding loop which was constructed near Stepford station. Until then the only connection between the quarry and the railway had been a steep road, which had hampered output efficiency. The ropeway, which was 400 yards long and supported by three steel trestles, carried eight buckets with the capacity to empty road metals at a rate of 20 tons per hour through a bunker into the railway wagons in the siding. Several of the navvies who had laboured on the building of the railway were taken on at the quarry, where they no doubt became intimately familiar with the workings of the ropeway and its endless cycle of buckets.

In 1909 the company finally gave up railmotor operations on the branch. The separation of engine and carriage had not been a great success while the passengers and the drivers were sick of the draughty cab and wet footplate, which was caused by the continual running of the tank overflow. David L. Smith recalled in his *Tales of the Glasgow and South-Western Railway* that the firebox and tubes of No. 3 were rumoured to have been burnt out and that for many years she lay derelict behind Dumfries engine shed where fresh apprentices were often sent to sweep her chimney. The company's two other railmotors worked the Catrine branch until it was closed temporarily in 1916. They were all sold for scrap in 1922.

Passenger services were taken over by one of James Manson's small '266' class 0-4-4 tank engines, No. 269. This design featured a short wheelbase for easier handling on the sharp bends found in shunting yards and rural branch lines. No. 269 was at Moniaive for little more than a year when it was involved in the most serious accident to occur on the branch.

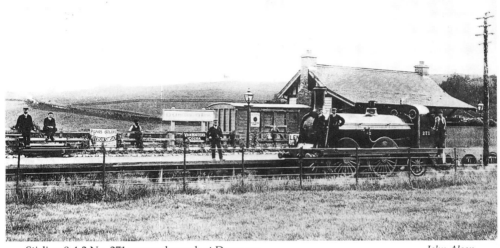

"Leisure Moments" — Dunscore Station, Cairn Valley, Railway.

Stirling 0-4-2 No. 271 on goods work at Dunscore.   *John Alsop*

Crossford station in 1905, the smart appearance of the travellers seems at odds with the basic facilities provided for their comfort.   *Christine Hiddleston*

Kirkland station and station house in 1905. *Dumfries Museums*

Moniaive station with George Macdonald and his staff assembled besides railmotor No. 3. A Stirling 0-4-2 is shunting in the yard. *Author's Collection*

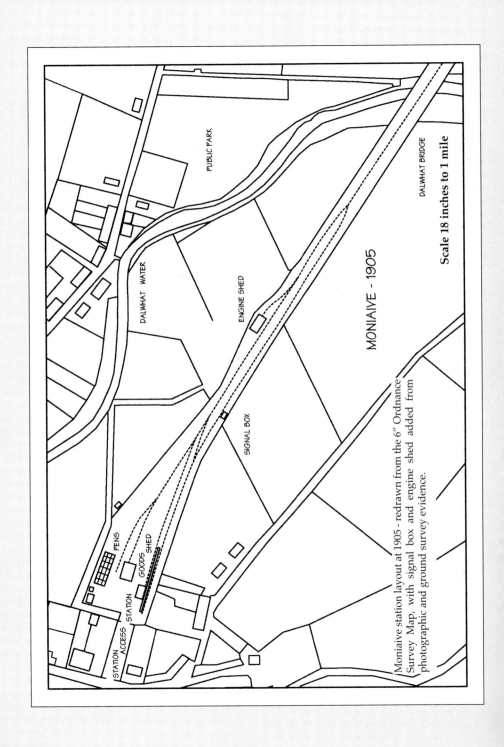

PUBLIC PARK

DALWHAT WATER

ENGINE SHED

SIGNAL BOX

DALWHAT BRIDGE

MONIAIVE - 1905

Scale 18 inches to 1 mile

PENS

GOODS SHED

STATION

ACCESS

STATION

Moniaive station layout at 1905 - redrawn from the 6" Ordnance Survey Map, with signal box and engine shed added from photographic and ground survey evidence.

A busy day at Moniaive - at least a dozen passengers and two dogs!
Stenlake Publishing, Dumfries & Galloway's Lost Railways

The Sykes' lock-and-block system relied greatly on the signalman to ensure safe operation and this drawback was highlighted in dramatic fashion on 6th January, 1911. The 10.45 am goods from Dumfries (rebuilt Stirling '221' class 0-4-2 No. 261) was sitting in the loop at Irongray waiting for No. 269 on the 10.40 am passenger service from Moniaive to go past, when Mr John Swan, the station master who also acted as signalman, reversed the points just as the passenger engine had reached them, sending her bunker first into No. 261.

The damage was quite extensive. The back wheels of No. 269 were lifted off the rails and her buffers pierced the guard's van. The buffers of both engines and of the passenger carriages were also badly twisted. Several of the passengers and crew were cut and bruised, however their injuries were slight, thanks to William McConnell, the driver of No. 269, who had realised that the engines were about to collide and had braked hard. The shaken passengers were taken into the station to await the arrival of a relief train from Dumfries.

A very fine view along the platform at Moniaive, taken about 1905.   *Author's Collection*

Right: Detailed view of Sykes' banner signal at Moniaive.

D. Barrie/*Railway Magazine*

Below: Signalling diagram for Irongray, Newtonairds and Dunscore.
Glasgow & South Western Railway Association

Bottom: Signalling diagram for Moniaive.
Glasgow & South Western Railway Association

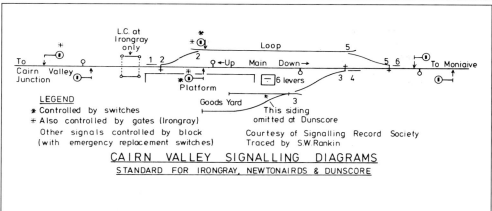

CAIRN VALLEY SIGNALLING DIAGRAMS
STANDARD FOR IRONGRAY, NEWTONAIRDS & DUNSCORE

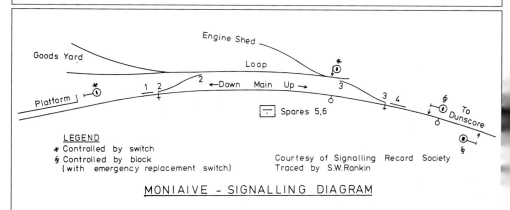

MONIAIVE - SIGNALLING DIAGRAM

Slide in Middle or Normal Position—Indicator Red.

A   **B**

Slide in "Out" Position, indicating Train   Slide in "In" Position, indicating Train
"A" to "B."   from "A."

Mode of Signalling.—For the purpose of illustrating the course to be adopted, *A* and *B* are supposed to represent each end of a Block Section, and the process of Signalling a Train is as follows :—

Prior to a Train being allowed to start from or pass *A*, the Signalman there, provided he has received *Train Out of Section* Signal for the previous Train, and the Indicators are in their normal position, must give the *Is Line Clear*

In the afternoon, the line superintendent, Mr Cockburn, travelled to the scene of the accident. Mr Swan freely admitted that in his eagerness to let the goods train leave as quickly as possible he had changed the points too soon and caused the collision. Mr Cockburn and the crash investigators seem to have accepted that the lack of in-built signalling protection had contributed to the accident as the station master kept his job. Mr Swan seems to have been accident prone for a year later he was caught between the buffers of a wagon and an engine and was lucky to escape with a head wound and a broken rib

While the passenger engine was under repair, another small Manson 0-4-4T, No. 332 of '326' class, came down from Glasgow to take over. These engines were intended originally for suburban services and it was very unusual for one to be seen on a rural branch line like the Cairn Valley.

In 1912, No. 232, a rebuilt Stirling '221' class 0-4-2, took over passenger work, and for many years ran tender-first down the valley. This class of engine also worked goods services and often were to be seen on sheep-specials until their withdrawal in the late 1920s. The railway was at its busiest during the lamb sales, as trains of 30 or more wagons - three times longer than usual - carried the flocks to Dumfries, Annan or Castle Douglas. This was also about the only time that two engines could be seen in Moniaive at once!

By October 1916, overall trade was considered good enough to warrant extending Moniaive station building to provide a separate office for the station master, and although passenger traffic slumped in 1917, it then improved until the end of the war. Around this time, No. 472, a rebuilt Stirling '191' class 4-4-0, was sent to work the branch and had its tender fitted with a weather-board to protect the crew from the elements when running backwards.

After 1919, the railway went into a steady decline and in 1921 the passenger service lost over £1,600. Moniaive engine shed was closed and from then on the first service of the day ran from Dumfries. In 1923, when the Glasgow and South-Western Railway Company was absorbed into the new LMS group, the line carried just 10,555 passengers, which meant that on average only about 35 people used the railway each day.

Station sign from Dumfries.   *Brian Hilton*

Chapter Five

Some Memories

The Cairn Valley Railway may never have been very important or busy, but these qualities have endeared it to the many people who have fond memories of the line. The relaxed nature of work on the branch also had its appeal for men with a bit of wit and imagination or interests outside the day-to-day confines of running a minor railway.

The first station master at Moniaive, Archibald Wilkie, was transferred to take charge of Kirkconnel station in 1907. He evidently was popular in Moniaive; the *Dumfries and Galloway Standard* reported that, to mark his departure, his friends and fellow employees presented him with 'a handsome marble timepiece with Corinthian columns and bronze figure plus a table lamp'.

However, the man who took Mr Wilkie's place became one of the best respected on the Cairn Valley line. This was Mr George Macdonald, who was originally from the Island of Mull where he trained as a teacher under the Church authorities. While still a young man he travelled to Glasgow where he joined the G&SW Company as a booking clerk and a few years later he was made up to chief clerk at Dumfries. He was promoted rapidly once more, this time to station master at Ruthwell, where he worked until taking up the same post at Moniaive. Mr Macdonald was a keen reader and student in English, French and his native Gaelic. Weather observations and astronomy were other major interests and he contributed many notes on the latter subject to the newspapers. Mr Macdonald was also a skilled gardener and the borders at Ruthwell and Moniaive won him so many first prizes that he was frequently barred from taking part in the company's horticultural competitions.

It was not only the station master who had a love of gardening. A.S. Alexander in his book *Tramps Across Watersheds* had the following to say about Moniaive and its station staff: 'The natives seemed cosy, canny, peaceful and probably pious. I overheard its workmen talking at the station as we awaited the train for Dumfries. The talk was of gardens and flowers and I thought how wholesome and enriching compared with the barren life and talk of town masses in confined conditions'.

The passenger train had the same crew for many years. Will McConnell, the driver, moved from Dumfries when the line opened and stayed at Moniaive until the engine shed was closed. His daughter lived right next to the line and his granddaughter remembers that this gave the fireman, Will Currie, the opportunity to throw the odd shovelful of coal into their back garden as the engine steamed past.

Like the station masters and signalmen, the crew worked long hours before the eight hour day came in. But they did get a break on Saturdays, when a Dumfries driver and fireman relieved them in the morning. The Moniaive men usually spent the afternoon at home and went back down to take over for the evening services. However, once during the Rood Fair in Dumfries the crew

Archibald Wilkie and his staff on the platform at Moniaive.

were watching the crowds spill out onto the platform when temptation got the better of them and they decided to stay and enjoy the festivities themselves. And so they did - but perhaps more than was prudent!

The driver and fireman were a bit the worse for wear by the time they reported back and the return journey was a struggle. The engine strained gallantly against the six or seven carriages that were needed at Fair time, but about a mile short of Moniaive she stuck for want of steam. No amount of tinkering could move her. As the crew worked away they noticed passengers leaving the train, and by the time one of them went to investigate he found that everyone had gone. The Moniaive folk had made their own way home and the crew decided that they might as well just do the same. They awoke with clearer heads the next morning and went back and brought their engine into the station. Since there were no Sunday services, and the passengers had been happy enough to get back by any means, the matter was never reported to the authorities.

Passengers going missing was bad enough, but one night in 1915 the crew excelled themselves by losing the whole train. At Moniaive the engine was shunting to the head of the 8.50 pm from Dumfries. However, unknown to the driver, the guard was not in his van, the brake had been left off and the carriages ran away. Douglas Macdonald, the station master's son, recorded in his diary that he had chased them as far as Kirkland before giving up and that the coaches had to be retrieved from about Crossford where they had finally rolled to a standstill.

Besides special occasions like the Fair, the busiest passenger service was the 'pictur train', which left for Dumfries around four o'clock on Saturdays, allowing time for an evening at the cinema before returning at nine. The non-corridor train had no toilets, which often caused delays in the small intermediate stations while those young men who had enjoyed a few 'refreshments' in the town's public houses jumped off to make their own arrangements. At times the train was obligingly backed-up to retrieve any wayward souls who had forgotten to get back on!

Wednesdays were also busy as this was market day in Dumfries. Mr R.O. Blair-Cunynghame had these memories of the market train and its timekeeping in the 1920s:

Our station master presided in his gold laced cap and frock coat, none of the modern short jacket for such an important functionary, at any rate not on a Wednesday morning. One carriage on the Wednesday's train was always reserved for our leading citizens, the chief merchant and the grain dealer, the bank agent and the village tailor whose business took them to Dumfries on a market day. Local farmers too, would drive to the station in their traps for a day's business in Dumfries, while their wives accompanied them to go shopping.

Actually, the train kept very good time, due, I think, rather to a very easy schedule, than to any turn of speed. For instance, the Wednesday train would never think of starting without one of the occupants of the banker's carriage, but in spite of these delays at departure, owing to the late arrival of one or other of the regulars, we always seemed to reach Dumfries on time. This was all the more remarkable as sometimes we had similar delays at stations *en route*. Mrs A would be seen running down the road to the station waving an umbrella or shouting to the station-master, Mr B from the farm had sent down to say that he was coming but a minute late owing to some agricultural crisis, eventually, however, all would be hoisted or pushed on board - our train had rather high running boards - and off we would go once more, accompanied by a running commentary from the carriages on local affairs.

Cynicus Publishing Company card extolling the virtues of the Moniaive motor bus.

Author's Collection

A similar treatment for the Moniaive railway. The message on the back of the card reads: 'I don't think you have anything in Glasgow to beat this!'   *Author's Collection*

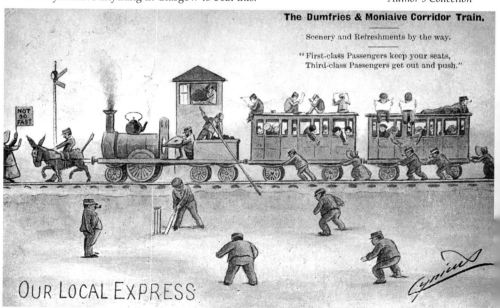

A Manson 0-4-4T running into Dunscore station with three carriages attached. This view dates from 1910.   *Author's Collection*

Busier times at Dunscore, as a Manson '266' class 0-4-4T arrives with a 'Fair' special of nine carriages.   *Author's Collection*

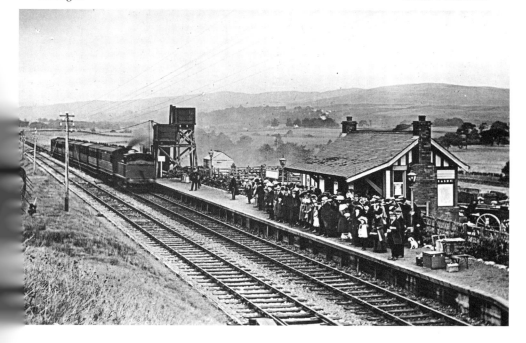

Yeomanry arriving at Moniaive station during World War I.

Mrs Hastings, Moniaive

The Moniaive area volunteers on parade at the station around 1914.   *Jock Black*

Herbert Buchanan boards the train at Moniaive. The start of a long journey to France and the
Western Front.   *Dumfries & Galloway Libraries, Information & Archives*

(622)

GLASGOW & SOUTH-WESTERN RAILWAY.

REFER TO

Mr/
344.

IN YOUR REPLY.

MONIAIVE _____ Station,

14th July 19 23.

Sir,

Reattached, the traffic in question was consigned & carried at Owner's Risk.

I cannot, therefore, entertain your claim, which I herewith return.

Yours truly,

R Macdonald.

Agent.

Graham F Macara. Esq.,
General Merchant.

A memo to grain dealer Graham F. Macara from Moniaive station.   *Jock Black*

The banker's carriage was in fact an ordinary third and the seats were reserved by habit rather than by any company decree. But woe betide anyone else who tried to sit there!

Other regular passengers on the railway were school children for Dumfries Academy. One lady who travelled to school each day from Dunscore between 1916 and 1918 recalled that there was plenty of room for fun and games as the seats were on either side of the train. Ken Rae, the guard, had great time for the children and checked that they were all aboard before the afternoon train left from Dumfries. She was sure that although at times there was lots of noise, there was never any vandalism. This same lady's sister travelled on the line in 1905 and remembered that the railmotor shook and rattled a great deal. Mr Blair-Cunynghame also had fond memories of Mr Rae, who he described as 'a lugubrious figure with a pessimistic walrus moustache'. Another with happy memories of the line is Henry Corrie, who as small boy was sent with his brothers for holidays with his grandparents at Burnbank Moniaive, right next to the station where, 'Looking down the garden to watch the trains come in and lying in our beds in the early morning and hearing the first train of the day working its way up the glen were amongst the highlights of our visits to Moniaive'.

Although the passenger services provided a barely adequate trade for the line, the regular contract with Morrinton quarry for transportation of road metals tended to make up for any losses. One of the main freight customers in Moniaive was Graham F. Macara, who ran a general supply store and owned several grain mills. A series of business letters to Mr Macara from 1923 show that trains to Moniaive and Dunscore were regularly carrying four ton wagonloads of oats, maize, bran and beans from merchants in Dumfries, Glasgow, Dundee, Carlisle, Yorkshire and beyond. The nature of the correspondence is usually to confirm dispatch of the required order, but one or two letters reveal that some transactions did not run altogether smoothly - especially with regard to arguments over carriage rates. For example on 23rd May, 1923, Alexander Cross & Sons Limited, Fertiliser Dealers, Glasgow, respond to a query from Mr Macara as follows:

Dear Sir,
    We have yours of 22nd with reference to the price of 17s. 3d. charged for rail carriage. You will notice that this has only been charged on the raw manures which are based on the Glasgow price, and 17s. 3d. is the four ton railway rate from Glasgow to Moniaive.
    We trust this will now make the matter quite clear to you.

Other disputes featured in these letters centre on responsibility for spoiled goods. No-one was keen to take the blame when compensation claims were being made. On 14th July, 1923 Mr Macdonald writes curtly from Moniaive station:

Sir,
    Re attached, the traffic in question was consigned at Owner's Risk. I cannot, therefore, entertain your claim, which I herewith return.

While on 23rd November, James Aitken & Sons, Grain & Flour Importers write:

> Regarding the 4 tons of Roumanian Maize sent you on 14th November which smells very strongly of benzel, we think this must have happened in the hands of the Railway Co., but we are writing the Granary today, and will let you know what they say.

Moniaive station yard was obviously an attraction to boys in the village, some for the pleasure of watching the engines shunt the yard, and others for more profitable reasons. The late Tom Todd recalled that as a boy of 12 in 1925, he collected clothes hampers off the trains and loaded them onto a barrow, which he pushed round to Moniaive hand laundry. The 3*d*. he received per hamper, and the packets of Woodbine cigarettes he spent it on, ensured that he was always popular with his schoolmates. Another who frequented the station yard as a lad was the late David Henderson, who, with his pals, would sometimes cadge a ride on the footplate of the goods engine. He especially remembered the stir caused one day when it was discovered that a train had gone straight through Crossford station, carrying the crossing gates with it!

The busiest time of the year for the goods service was during late summer when the lamb sales took place. Mr Blair-Cunynghame described the scene as follows:

> The village was a place of interest on these occasions, because at the cross at the centre of the village the main road was joined by the station road, which provided endless possibilities, especially when two flocks of sheep converged from opposite ends of the village, both of which had to be turned up the station road one at a time, while more flocks pressed on their heels behind.
>
> The efforts to get them turned one at a time towards the station, without getting them intermingled, used to keep us enthralled for hours, especially as the lambs were for the most part straight off the hills and quite unused to human habitations, to say nothing of being young and able to jump like stags. Shepherds and dogs, assisted by the villagers with time to spare, or who had made time to spare, were all heavily engaged particularly at the road junction.
>
> I can still remember the shepherds whistled instructions to the dogs, a confused bleating, shouts of 'Hoo! Ha! Ha!' from the arm-waving villagers and a heavy smell of sheep all over the street. Occasionally the sturdy hill lambs would dodge the outstretched arms or take a flying leap over a low held stick; to be hotly pursued by a large posse of volunteers and disentangled from neighbouring flocks and finally routed for the station.

The slow pace of life in the valley seemed to rub off on everyone connected with the railway, including the crew of the goods train, as Mr Blair-Cunynghame went on to describe:

> There was too, I believe good fishing to be had from the train, rumour had it that the goods engine carried a fishing rod in the tender and during its lengthy pauses to pick up a truck or two at each station, there was ample opportunity for one of the engine crew to do a little fishing while the other shunted the train.

However, these lighter moments did not produce any revenue for the company and as the years between the wars wore on the future of the line began to look increasingly bleak.

Chapter Six

Decline and Closure

The first sign that the Cairn Valley line was not going to live up to the original forecasts for its success came only seven months after the opening ceremony. At the G&SW's half-yearly general meeting, Mr Charlton of Dumfries stated that the new railway would never again carry as many passengers over a similar period as it had in those first few months and that it would be pointless building a special bay platform at Dumfries to serve the Cairn Valley line as had been proposed initially. The company seems to have taken Mr Charlton's advice as the bay was never constructed and the Cairn Valley trains always used the main platforms.

However, rather than the amount of trade, the weather was often of more immediate concern to the men who had to work the railway.

In bad winters, snow was a problem on exposed parts of the line; for instance, there were severe disruptions to services during January 1913. The 2.05 pm goods train from Moniaive managed to get through the snow without any difficulty until it ran into a large drift at Snadeford and stuck fast. A breakdown train hauled by two engines was summoned and after several hours' work the goods train was dug out and brought forward to Dunscore. While this was happening, a passenger service shuttled between Dumfries and Dunscore, where travellers for further up the valley were forced to wait. The line was cleared about one o'clock on Sunday morning and the passenger train eventually reached Moniaive 40 minutes later. The Moniaive poultry show had taken place on the Saturday and there was a large number of visitors anxious to get back to Dumfries. Many had waited with friends in the village, while others passed the time by singing in the station waiting room. The folk waiting in the village were alerted that a train had made it through and all the passengers left for home at 1.45 am.

The closeness of the track to the Cluden and Cairn waters meant that there was always a high risk of flooding during heavy rain. At Crossford and over the last mile before Moniaive, the land was very low lying, and even though the line was built up on embankments the water often came close to covering them over. For example George Macdonald recorded in his diary for 4th November, 1918 that he was 'very late on duty on account of wash out at Bridge 38, Jarbruck. Heaviest flood since we came to Moniaive'.

Mr Macdonald's diaries also provide an insight into other everyday difficulties encountered in running a small rural station. The entry for 8th April, 1914 reveals 'office broken into last night'. The *Dumfries and Galloway Standard* reported that the burglars firstly had broken into a surfaceman's hut, where they had stolen tools which they used to force their way into the booking offices at Moniaive, Dunscore and Newtonairds, before escaping with about £6. A recurring problem was the lack of gas at Moniaive station. This crops up in entries for 2nd December, 1914, 'No gas'; 8th December, 1914, 'Still no gas'; and for 24th-27th December, 1918, 'Gas after a year's absence'.

Stirling '221' class 0-4-2 No. 17067 with a mixed train heading for Cairn Valley Junction and Moniaive in the 1920s.   *Scottish Records Office/British Railways Board*

Engine No. 14258, a Manson '240' class 4-4-0, heading a train of one carriage at Moniaive in 1930.
L&GRP

Although bad weather, break-ins and lack of gas were no doubt disruptive enough, an entry in Mr Macdonald's diary, describing a special livestock train, reveals a more ominous threat to the railway: 'Up at 4.40 am, only 5 wagons, MacMillan's 3 had gone by road'. The increasing reliability and availability of petrol-driven vehicles meant that lorries started to attract more goods traffic, while motor-buses became serious competition for the railway's passenger service, which by the end of World War I had been reduced to two return trips on weekdays.

By the mid-1920s, the South of Scotland Motor Company was running a bus four times daily between Moniaive and Dumfries, and the LMS in turn increased its service to four trains to Dumfries and three back to Moniaive. Ten years later the Caledonian Bus Company had seven runs per day during the week with extra buses at the weekend, including Sundays, while the LMS service had only added an early-morning train from Dumfries, which could not have attracted very many passengers.

Cairn Valley Timetable September 1935

Dumfries-Moniaive

			SO			SO
	am	am	pm	pm	pm	pm
Dumfries	6.52	8.38	12.20	2.44	5.17	9.00
Irongray	7.05	8.51	12.33	2.57	5.30	9.13
Newtonairds	7.12	8.58	12.40	3.05	5.37	9.20
Stepford	7.17	9.03	12.45	3.10	5.42	9.25
Dunscore	7.22	9.08	12.50	3.15	5.47	9.30
Crossford	7.31	9.17	12.59	3.24	5.56	9.39
Kirkland	7.38	9.23	1.06	3.31	6.03	9.46
Moniaive	7.44	9.29	1.12	3.37	6.09	9.52

Moniaive-Dumfries

			SO			SO
	am	am	pm	pm	pm	pm
Moniaive	7.50	9.37	1.22	3.50	6.17	10.05
Kirkland	7.57	9.44	1.29	3.57	6.24	10.12
Crossford	8.04	9.51	1.36	4.04	6.31	10.18
Dunscore	8.13	10.00	1.45	4.13	6.40	10.27
Stepford	8.18	10.05	1.50	4.18	6.46	10.33
Newtonairds	8.23	10.10	1.55	4.23	6.52	10.39
Irongray	8.30	10.17	2.02	4.30	7.00	10.47
Dumfries	8.43	10.30	2.15	4.43	7.13	11.00

SO - Saturday only

The railway was fighting a losing battle. Besides offering a better timetable the buses had the advantage that they would call almost at the passengers' doorsteps, whereas most of the stations on the Cairn Valley line were quite far away from the villages or farms that they were meant to serve. The number of passengers using the railway began to fall dramatically and only the Saturday trains were likely to be reasonably busy.

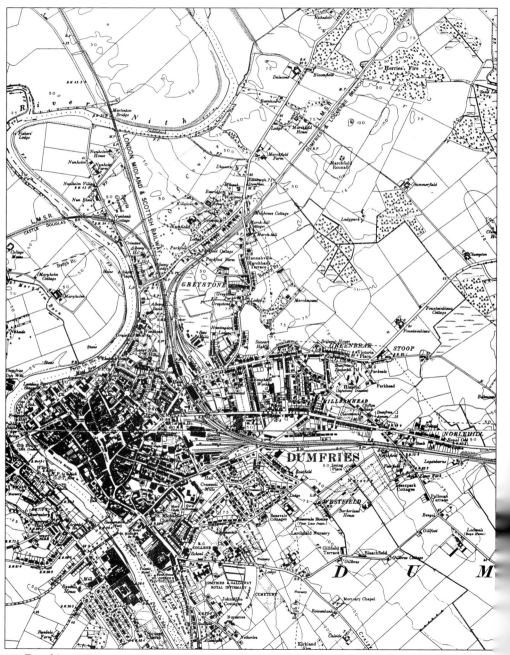

Dumfries station.   *Reproduced from the 6", 1933 Ordnance Survey Map*

An overview of Dumfries station taken in 1931. *L&GRP*

A 1930s view of Irongray station looking towards Dumfries. *Lens of Sutton*

The Cairn in flood at Gaups Mill about a mile before Moniaive. It's easy to see how the river could be a threat to the railway.   *Author's Collection*

A view of Dunscore from the 1930s. Even after the railway's heyday the stations were obviously well maintained.   *Lens of Sutton*

Former G&SW locomotives could be seen working the branch during this period, including No. 472 (by then LMS No. 14231) in 1924, Manson '240' class 4-4-0 No. 14258 in 1930 and Whitelegg-rebuilt Manson '361' class 0-6-0 No. 17485 in 1932. A standard LMS class '2P' locomotive, No. 603, was noted in 1934, but thereafter the line was worked by ex-Caledonian Railway 0-6-0 engines, normally hauling only one coach. Mr Peter Imrie of Dumfries worked on the branch in 1938, firing to veteran G&SW drivers whose names he recalled as Boyd, Rogerson, Keenan and Naysmith. He remembered that the run was fairly easy for the fireman because the passenger trains were small and the guard worked all the sidings and some crossings. The largest trains he encountered consisted of about 15 wagons which were run to and from the quarry sidings at Stepford.

Although the speed limit on the line was supposedly 25 mph, Mr E.R. McCarter reported in the *Railway Magazine* that he had occasionally recorded between 40 and 45 mph during the 1930s. He added that trains often arrived early at intermediate stations and had to wait until the scheduled time for departure and that, just before the outbreak of World War II, the last train on Saturday nights left Moniaive at 10.05 pm, called only at Dunscore and arrived at Dumfries at 10.45 pm, providing the nearest thing to an express service ever seen on the line.

Around 1936 the LMS removed the Sykes' signals and control gear and the line was worked by means of a brass Key Token between Cairn Valley Junction and a Train Staff Key from Dunscore to Moniaive. A replacement set of signals was erected at Dunscore where trains could cross, and from Dunscore to Moniaive the line was operated on the principle of 'one engine in steam'. Thereafter the crossing loops at Irongray and Newtonairds should not have been necessary, and the loop at Irongray was indeed removed, but the loop at Newtonairds was left in place, as were the signal boxes at both stations. The sidings on the line were worked by the original ground frames, which were modified such that they could be operated by the Key Token between Cairn Valley Junction and Dunscore, and the Staff Key between Dunscore and Moniaive. Clear instructions were issued that no trains should be permitted to pass by using these sidings.

The last large numbers of passengers to travel on the line were Norwegian troops moving to and from their camps near Moniaive and Dunscore during the war. The ordinary passenger service again fell to two trains in each direction from Monday to Friday, with only one extra return trip on Saturdays. However, the lack of traffic, together with the valley's seclusion, made the branch ideal for occasional use as a 'sleeping siding' when military commanders or other VIPs were travelling in Scotland.

Cairn Valley Timetable September 1942

	am	*SO* *pm*	*pm*		*am*	*SO* *pm*	*pm*
Dumfries	6.25	12.22	5.15	Moniaive	7.30	1.24	6.15
Irongray	6.40	12.35	5.29	Kirkland	7.37	1.31	6.22
Newtonairds	6.47	12.42	5.36	Crossford	7.44	1.38	6.29
Stepford	6.52	12.47	5.41	Dunscore	7.53	1.47	6.38
Dunscore	6.57	12.52	5.46	Stepford	7.58	1.52	6.44
Crossford	7.06	1.01	5.55	Newtonairds	8.04	1.57	6.50
Kirkland	7.12	1.08	6.02	Irongray	8.11	2.04	6.58
Moniaive	7.18	1.14	6.08	Dumfries	8.24	2.17	7.11

SO - Saturday only

Two views of the last passenger train from Moniaive, the 6.15 pm on the 1st May, 1943, hauled by ex-CR 0-6-0 No. 17405. *E.R. McCarter/Railway Magazine*

This scene could almost be believable on the last run after the Fair. The back of the card reads: 'We hope to travel on this line on Thursday but hope to guard against the rush!'
Author's Collection

At Moniaive on Saturday 1st May, 1943, a few people boarded the 6.15 pm train headed by ex-CR 0-6-0 No. 17405, which pulled out of the station and disappeared slowly into the distance towards Dumfries for the last time. Passenger trains were withdrawn officially from 3rd May until at least the end of the war. In contrast to the railway's opening day, the event passed without any ceremony. The local papers did not even publish a notice of the line's closure; the world was in turmoil and there was no time for sentiment at the passing of a minor branch line. The LMS Fortnightly Notice for 6th May, 1943, declared that:

> Goods, Minerals and Live Stock traffics in full loads will continue to be dealt with at the Stations on the Branch.
> Parcels and Sundry Goods traffic for conveyance from or to Moniaive, Kirkland and Crossford will be dealt with at Moniaive and similar traffic from or to Dunscore, Stepford, Newtonairds and Irongray will be dealt with at Irongray.

Around that time the railway lost the Morrinton quarry contract to road haulage and total closure began to look inevitable.

Although the passenger service was never reinstated, the daily goods train did carry a few railway enthusiasts who had sensed that there was little time left if they hoped to travel on the branch. One of these visitors was Mr G.H. Robin, who described the journey he made on 18th April, 1949 in the G&SW Railway Association's Journal.

Mr Robin recorded that the train was hauled by an old ex-Caledonian engine, No. 57378, which set off up the valley at a very leisurely pace. He also noted that besides Dunscore station the line was quiet and that the crew had to work all the level crossing gates themselves, except at Snadeford, where an elderly lady obliged by opening and closing the barriers in both directions. The line was showing signs of neglect and the shelter at Kirkland station had been demolished, but Mr Robin thought that the remaining buildings still had an air of neatness. The branch timetable had always been flexible, but with only one train per day it had become practically non-existent; for instance, when Moniaive was reached, the guard told Mr Robin to take his time in the village as the crew would just sit and wait for him! On a pay day his wait could have been lengthy as the crew would often retire to the bar of Craigdarroch Arms Hotel for the afternoon before running the train back to Dumfries.

Not long after Mr Robin made his trip, British Railways instigated a review of returns and staffing levels at certain Scottish rural stations, one of which was Moniaive. In the Glasgow Office of the operating superintendent, the Moniaive file was handed to Matthew McNaught, who given the low usage figures from the line, had little option but to recommend that the goods service should be withdrawn. This was a poignant moment for Mr McNaught, who was Moniaive born-and-bred and had started his railway career in the booking office there with the G&SW before promotion took him to Glasgow. However, in early May Moniaive Community Council petitioned BR to keep the branch open for a month's trial to see if traffic would increase. The service was retained but reduced to three trains per week. Some local councillors had visions of branch lines such as the Cairn Valley Railway providing a coordinated means of

Ex-Caledonian Railway 'Jumbo' No. 57378 shunting a load of timber at Stepford, 18th April, 1949.   *George Robin/The Mitchell Library*

No. 57378 drawn up at the platform at Dunscore. Note the replacement set of signals by the water tank.   *George Robin/The Mitchell Library*

The view from above the cab of No. 57378 running into Moniaive.

George Robin/The Mitchell Library

The crew of the same train at Moniaive: driver Willie Scott, guard J. Blackstock and fireman Stevenson. *George Robin/The Mitchell Library*

Irongray station looking towards Moniaive with No. 17405 on goods, 11th May, 1949.

J.L. Stevenson

No. 17405 is seen at the platform at Newtonairds on the branch goods, 11th May, 1949.

J.L. Stevenson

General view of Newtonairds from the road overbridge. No. 17405 shunts in the siding.
J.L. Stevenson

moving fresh produce to market and also acting as feeder lines for commuters to centres such as Dumfries. These thoughts were echoed in the *Standard's* 'Notes & Comments' of 7th May, 1949 which under the heading 'The Moniaive Express' stated:

> Now that the government own both the railways and the road transports, there should be better distribution of traffic, and the branch railway lines may again come into use. At present there is too much heavy long-distance traffic on the roads which could be diverted to the railways. Two immediate benefits would accrue from an intelligent organisation of road and rail traffic: the roads would be made safer and their maintenance less expensive.

During this period, Mr James Stevenson visited the branch to add to his collection of photos of the Scottish railway system. These bear out Mr Robin's description of the line, showing No. 17405 on one of the last goods trains standing at empty and slightly rundown-looking stations. The tin shelter at Crossford was particularly dilapidated with hardly any trace of the station platform to be seen.

Despite the aspirations of the Community Council and the *Standard*, which had followed the fortunes of the railway since it was first proposed in the 1860s, the line was closed for good on Monday 4th July, 1949. The *Standard's* final report on the line described the new arrangements for road and rail transfer of goods to and from Moniaive as follows:

> Truck load consignments will be conveyed by rail to or from the appropriate railhead - at Dumfries, Auldgirth or Thornhill - and between the railhead and the senders' or consignees' premises by vehicles of the Road Transport Executive.
>
> Freight train traffic in less than truck load consignments and parcels and miscellaneous traffic will be controlled by rail to or from Dumfries Station and between that station and the senders' or consignees' premises by vehicles of the Road Transport Executive.

A very similar view of Stepford station to that dating from 1910 (*see page 44*), except the the passenger shed has gone.   *J.L. Stevenson*

A detailed view of the water tanks and signals at the Dumfries side of Dunscore, 11th May, 1949.
                                                                                                                J.L. Stevenson

Dunscore station showing water tanks on the Moniaive side and rear view of goods train hauled by No. 17405. *J.L. Stevenson*

Crossford station with tin shelter still intact and station house in the background. *J.L. Stevenson*

No. 17405 shunting at Moniaive, 11th May, 1949.   *J.L. Stevenson*

A general view of the track layout at Moniaive.   *J.L. Stevenson*

A view of the empty platform at Moniaive, soon to be empty for good.   *J.L. Stevenson*

No. 17405 shunted to the head of the train at Moniaive ready to leave for Dumfries on 11th May, 1949.   *J.L. Stevenson*

Ex-Caledonian Railway 'Jumbo' No. 57349 with a train of flat trucks on demolition work near Irongray, 20th September, 1952.   *The late Derek Cross*

Demolition gang at work on a bridge on the Cairn Valley Railway. *From left to right*: J. Hepburn, R. Hardie, W. McMillan, S. Todd, W. Pitt, I. Templeton and W. McKeen.   *Sam Todd*

In the same way that the buses had robbed the line of its passenger trade, lorries and vans had killed off the goods service. Country people tend to be pragmatic, and the loss of the Cairn Valley Railway was accepted with regret, but also as part of natural progress. Mr Blair-Cunynghame summed his feelings up in this way:

> It served its turn and in any case, was lucky to have been built at all. Now we go by car or a regular and more or less frequent service of motor-buses; goods, livestock and feeding stuffs come and go by lorry. In spite of a bit of fuss when the line was finally closed, I am sorry to say that we can't feel that we have suffered much inconvenience. The gap is only a sentimental one and soon a generation will grow up who never knew our train.
>
> I'd like to think though that once a year, at midnight say on the anniversary of the line's closing, the rails appear again, the stations are occupied and that one might hear a ghostly clank and puff, and the sound of a whistle warning the wraiths of the old horse-drawn farm carts at the field crossings.

During the winter of 1949 long stretches of the track were washed out by floods and BR decided that the line should be demolished. The very last trains ran in the early 1950s to collect the rails and sleepers after they had been lifted, leaving the track bed to grass over. On completion of demolition, Cairn Valley Junction signal box was closed on 28th June, 1953. Although the track was lifted, the bridges on the line were left standing and farmers made use of these until they were no longer safe and had to be knocked down.

Today, the route of the railway can still be made out quite easily from the remaining cuttings and embankments, and the former crossing keepers' and station masters' houses, which have been maintained as private residences. The only intact bridge is the three-span viaduct near Dunscore, which is now overgrown with trees. All the stations have gone, except at Moniaive, where the booking office and goods shed now serve as farm sheds. The goods shed suffered badly in the Boxing Day storm of 1998 and lost quite a lot of its roof, which has since been repaired.

So the railway has had its day, and although, incredible as it may seem, there were serious moves afoot in late 1994 to resurrect it, the Cairn Valley will surely never again echo to the steam engine's whistle of Mr Blair-Cunynghame's dreams. The railway was built too late to have any real chance of success against road traffic, and the proposed connections to Ayr or Galloway were nothing more than pipe dreams, as were the hopes that Moniaive might become a busy and fashionable health resort. Even if the line had struggled on through the 1950s, the Beeching cuts would certainly have seen it closed, just like the stations at Thornhill and Auldgirth, which were its other proposed destinations when a railway was fought for all those years ago.

Perhaps the Cairn Valley line is best summed up as a railway that was used by ordinary people doing fairly ordinary things, and although the people of Moniaive may not miss it, they certainly remember it, try asking anyone there where the 'Station Yard' is - they'll be sure to know.

Appendix One

Glencairn Railway Prospectus, 1880

1. The Railway commences at the town of Moniaive, in the Parish of Glencairn, follows the course of the Cairn Water to a point near Dunscore Village, and thence to a junction at Auldgirth Station with the main line of the Glasgow and South-Western Railway from Glasgow to Dumfries and Carlisle.

2. The length of the line is about 10½ miles, and it has been laid out and surveyed by the Engineer as a single line of railway with the view to its economical construction. The works are of an unusually light character, with the exception of one bridge over the Nith, and a few yards of adjoining embankment - many miles of the road being practically level.

3. Arrangements of a satisfactory character have been made with the proprietors and tenants of the land required to be taken for the construction of the Line and Stations, by which the expenses attendant upon disputed settlements will be avoided, and a large proportion of them have also agreed to take payment of the sums found due to them in shares of the Company.

4. The necessary Parliamentary Powers for the construction of the line have been obtained, and the Directors have effected arrangements with the Promoters, by which the preliminary and Parliamentary expenses incurred in obtaining the Acts, and also all engineering expenses, have been fixed, and tenders have been received, from which the Directors are enabled to say that the whole works, including Permanent Way, Land, Stations, and Furnishings, will be completed for £65,000 or less than £6,000 a mile.

5. The sources from which the Railway will derive its principal support are well populated, extensive and highly-cultivated agricultural and pastoral districts held by a wealthy proprietary, and a substantial and enterprising class of tenants, and the Railway will not only be of great advantage to the proprietors in the district, but it is believed that, taking a moderate of the revenue, a fair return will be obtained for the capital expended ; and that, too, immediately on the Line being opened for traffic.

6. The undertaking has been well received in the district, and subscriptions have already intimated to the amount of nearly £40,000. The Directors of the Glasgow and South-Western Railway Company will be prepared, on the necessary capital being subscribed, to enter into an agreement to supply plant and work the line, and to give every facility for the development of its traffic.

7. Subscriptions will be received up till Thursday, 28th July, 1880. Forms of application for Shares may be obtained by applying to JOHN MORTON, Esq., Secretary, St Enoch Station, Glasgow, or to the Brokers or Solicitors.

St Enoch Station, Glasgow, 13th July, 1880.

Appendix Two

Memorandum on
Moniaive Railway Proposals

The following notes are abridged from the Moniaive deputation's memorandum which was presented to the G&SW on 6th October, 1896.

Moniaive, which is nine miles from Thornhill Station, is the centre of a large district, comprising the Parish of Glencairn and parts of the Parishes of Tynron, Carsphairn, Dalry and, Balmaclellan, the valuation of which may be put at over £29,000, while the population is about 2,500, Glencairn itself being the most highly valued agricultural parish in Dumfriesshire.

The land is held by a large number of proprietors, a very considerable majority of whom reside on their properties, and expend locally, in many cases, a much greater sum than they receive locally.

As a summer resort and for sport, this district is coming into greater favour every year.

At present its prosperity is severely interfered with by its want of quick and cheap communication with the market town and railway centre of Dumfries.

Except on Wednesday (the market day), when the journey can be made in two hours and ten minutes the one way and three hours on return, at a fare of 3s. 6d. (distance by road 16 miles), the transit from Moniaive to Dumfries occupies three hours and ten minutes, and the fare is 5s. This obviously prevents to a great extent produce being taken or sent to Dumfries, and equally prevents goods and supplies coming from Dumfries to the district, as cartage is a correspondingly great expense.

At present large numbers of store sheep and cattle are sent out of the district by road, which with proper railway facilities would proceed by rail. Fat stock, wool, and wood are also dealt with in great quantity, but trade in the last-named is at a standstill through lack of means of carriage. For the same reason dairy farming is greatly checked, but might be largely and profitably developed.

There is continual and important importation of coal, feeding stuffs, manures, and general stores.

A suitable railway would at once secure a large amount of business, which would rapidly increase, as there would almost certainly ensue a growth of population and, with enterprise, of tourist traffic.

It is the very firm persuasion of those who have lived all their life in the district, and are intimately acquainted with its needs and resources, that the only line of railway which would fully meet the necessities of the case, and give the prospect of financial success, would be one running down the easy and beautiful valley of the Cairn. The inhabitants of Moniaive district, who will be most affected by a line of Railway, are practically unanimous in favour of this route.

The following reasons may be given for the above statement:

1. ENGINEERING

(a) No difficulties would be encountered. Moniaive stands about 320 feet higher than Dumfries but the elevation is attained by a gradual rise spread over 16 miles.
(b) Except the Cairn (called near Dumfries the Cluden), there is no stream and there are few roads to be crossed.
(c) The line would be well sheltered in winter.

2.   PUBLIC ADVANTAGE

The line, which would not come within 4½ miles of any existing railway station till near Dumfries, would open up a new territory, which would comprise, in addition to the district above described, large portions of the Parishes of Holywood, Dunscore, Irongray and Kirkpatrick Durham, in all of which the distinguishing feature of Glencairn is maintained - resident landowners and large mansion houses. The territory is at present peculiarly badly situated with regard to railway communication.

By this line the distance from Moniaive to Dumfries would not exceed 17 miles, and throughout would traverse country of great natural beauty and historical interest.

3.   FINANCIAL CONSIDERATIONS

(a)   Expense of construction would be the minimum.
(b)   The great bulk of the traffic of the Moniaive district would be secured. As a considerable part thereof now goes by road to Dumfries this would be very largely new traffic.
(c)   It is believed that the landowners on this route would in no case oppose, but the most influential of them would facilitate the construction of the line.
(d)   The district served by the railway would be much richer and more populous than the district to be referred to below. What is true regarding new traffic in the Moniaive district is still more true of the district between Dunscore and Dumfries.
(e)   A line from Dumfries to Moniaive might at some future time be extended into Ayrshire for more than one reason

It is understood that an Alternative Route from Moniaive to Thornhill by Penpont has been suggested. To the suggestion the following Objections are taken:

1.   ENGINEERING

(a)   Between Thornhill and Moniaive a watershed has to be crossed, involving a total rise of some 215 feet and then a total fall of some 112 feet in 9 miles ; but at one point there would be a rise of 200 feet in 1¼ miles (gradient of 1 in 33).
(b)   A viaduct or bridge, with approaches, must be constructed over the Nith; and the Scaur, Shinnel, and Dalwhat water must also be bridged. Several roads would have to be crossed - one of them several times.
(c)   The line would be badly exposed to winter storms at its most difficult point.
(d)   A large and expensive alteration would need to be made on Thornhill Station.

2.   PUBLIC ADVANTAGE

While Penpont parish would be distinctly benefited, as well as a part of Keir, and to a questionable extent, Tynron, this line would be manifestly much less convenient for the Moniaive district than the other, while for the lower part of Glencairn, and thence to Dumfries, it would be useless.

There would be a change of train at Thornhill; passengers would not be able there to change into the fastest trains.

While for 11 or 12 miles of its length the Cairn Valley line would not be within 4.5 miles of an existing railway station, the line to Thornhill would be for one half of its whole length of 9 miles within 4½ miles of that station.

3.   FINANCIAL CONSIDERATIONS

(a)   It is believed that, though the line to Thornhill would be shorter than that to Dumfries by several miles, it would cost a very much larger sum per mile, and there would be far less chance of adequate return on the capital employed.
(b)   A large amount of traffic in the Moniaive district would continue to go to Dumfries direct by road (16 miles) rather than incur the expenditure of money and time involved in going round by Thornhill (23 miles).
(c)   The Thornhill line would not attract traffic from any new district whatever.
(d)   The line would pass for half its length through the land of one proprietor, who is non-resident, and for a third of its length through the land of proprietors who, though resident, are strongly opposed to its construction.

Names and Members of Deputation to the Directors of the Glasgow and South-Western Railway Company - 6th October, 1896.

REV. SIR EMILIUS LAURIE Bart., of Maxwelton.
JAMES McCALL of Caitloch (Glencairn) and Bogrie (Dunscore).
WILLIAM BARBER of Terreran, C.C.
REV. P. M. PLAYFAIR, Chairman Glencairn Parish Council.
ALEX. CRAIG, factor to Colonel Sir George G. Walker K.C.B., of Crawfordton.
JOHN MILLIGAN of Merkland (Dunscore) and Garrieston (Glencairn), C.C., Chairman of Dunscore Parish Council.
REV. R SIMPSON, Dunscore.
THOMAS MOFFAT of Sunnyhill, Holywood.
PROVOST GLOVER, Dumfries.
DEAN HIDDLESTON, Dumfries.
R. McMILLAN of Holm of Dalquairn, Carsphairn.
J.W.F. CONNELL of Auchencheyne.
R. ADAMSON, W.S., Chairman Irongray Parish Council.

Appendix Three

Memorial on
Moniaive to Thornhill Railway

The following notes are abridged from the Thornhill deputation's memorial which was submitted to the G&SW on 30th October, 1896.

MEMORIAL

To the Directors of the Glasgow and South-Western Railway Company, submitted on behalf of the Parishes of Morton, Penpont, Keir, and Tynron, regarding extension of Line from Thornhill to Moniaive.

GENTLEMEN,

On behalf of our constituents in the Parishes of Morton, Penpont, Keir, and Tynron, we desire to submit to you the following statement in support of the proposed line of railway from Thornhill to Moniaive.

We have to inform you that during the past week largely attended and most enthusiastic public meetings have been held in Thornhill (for Morton Parish), in Penpont (for Penpont and Keir Parishes), and in Tynron (for Tynron Parish), and at each of these meetings a resolution was submitted and carried unanimously, and with acclamation, urging the desirability of the line of railway proposed, and the great public benefit such an extension would be. The following delegates were appointed at these meetings to wait on you in Glasgow, and urge on you the feeling of the public in the districts referred to , viz:

MORTON PARISH - Messrs John H. Dickson, Dabton, Chamberlain to His Grace the Duke of Buccleuch ; James Milligan, Hayfield, J. P., Chairman of the Nithsdale Auction Co., Ltd. ; Alexander Kirkpatrick, Bacon Factor ; and Robert Thomson, Quarrymaster.

PENPONT PARISH - Messrs Robert Dalziel, Druidhall, J. P., and Thomas R. Haddow, Merkland, C. C.

KEIR PARISH - Messrs James Stobo, Porterstown, C. C., and Hugh H. Allan, Beuchan.

TYNRON PARISH - Messrs Stephen Brown, Bennan, and James Laurie, Merchant.

We, the delegates beforenamed, desire, therefore, to submit to you now the principal arguments we have to adduce in favour of the proposed line, that you may have an opportunity of reviewing these before we appear before you in support of them, thus, to a great extent, obviating the necessity of recapitulating them verbally, and, at the same time, permitting you by pertinent interrogations to clear up any point that may be obscure, or to obtain fuller information where you may deem it necessary or desirable.

With reference to the three proposed routes:

1. The 'Clone' Route.

This route has been fully surveyed. the survey proceeds from Thornhill by way of Stepends to Penpont, thence through Grennan Estate to Ford, thence skirting the top of the Glen to Shancastle, and onwards through Colonel Sir George Walker's Estate to Moniaive. For the first 5½ miles the proprietors of the land on this route are known to be favourable towards the proposed line, and the proprietors of the remaining 3½ miles are at present advocating the alternative line to Dumfries hereafter referred to.

2. The Tynron Route.

This route has been partially surveyed. The survey would follow that of No. 1 to Shinnel, thence up the Shinnel Water to Tynron Village and across Dunreggan to Moniaive. The proprietors along this route (viz : His Grace the Duke of Buccleuch ; James Hewetson, Esquire of Grennan ; James J. Mein Austin, Esquire of Dalmakerran ; and Steuart Gladstone, Esquire of Lann Hall) are all known to be in favour of the proposed line of railway.

3. The Cairn Valley Route.

This proposal is to proceed from Moniaive to Dumfries, joining the main line at or near the station of Holywood. The line must necessarily pass through the lands of numerous small proprietors, who are not known to be in favour of such a railway.

YOUR MEMORIALISTS propose now to deal generally with the main features of the projected line from Thornhill to Moniaive. The feeling in the district, as strongly evinced by the public meetings referred to, is the first and best argument to be submitted. It seems to be the universal desire that a railway extension from Thornhill to Moniaive should be made. The want of such an extension has been felt for years, but it is only within a more recent period the need has become so acutely felt, and this is evidenced by the perpetual stream of traffic which now daily passes along the road between Thornhill and Moniaive. It is believed the construction of the line proposed would be the means of largely developing the present trade of the district, and probably creating new industries.

Sources of New Traffic

Large freestone quarries exist near Thornhill Station, at present employing close on a hundred hands, and were railway facilities obtained, there is every probability that a large amount of stone would pass along the proposed line. The present cost of cartage of stone from these quarries is 1s. 8d. per ton to Thornhill; 4s. per ton to Penpont ; and 8s. per ton to Moniaive ; and this heavy charge has naturally a deterrent effect on building enterprise in the district. His Grace the Duke of Buccleuch has recently granted feuing facilities to the public in and around Thornhill, which have already been largely taken advantage of; and your memorialists have reason to believe that a great impetus would be given to the building trade were fast trains to stop at Thornhill. The beauty of the scenery in the neighbourhood is unrivalled in the south of Scotland. There is excellent fishing and shooting in the district, and each year finds a large influx of sportsmen and visitors.

Large tracts of larch and other wood are to be found in the district, and there is at present one sawmill in Tynron parish, lying close to the proposed route, capable of considerable development.

In Keir parish there are valuable and extensive lime-kilns, and the quality of the lime is said to be unsurpassed in Scotland.

An auction mart, doing a considerable trade, has been constructed close to Thornhill Station in recent years, and were the proposed line carried out it would tap a large and excellent grazing area, both along its course and also at its terminus, and farmers and dealers in the district would send their stock by rail to and from the mart in preference to driving them along the road, as they do at present.

There are large dairies in the parishes of Penpont, Keir, Tynron, Glencairn, and, were railway facilities more readily obtainable, the farmers would undoubtedly send much more milk to Glasgow and other large centres than they do at present.

All mineral traffic and nearly all traffic in feeding-stuffs and other merchandise, come from the north and west at present. The bulk of the passenger traffic also proceeds westward, and these facts are strong arguments in favour of the route advocated by your Memorialists.

The population of the various parishes which the proposed railway would trench on is as follows:

Morton		1,852
Penpont		1,065
Keir		745
Tynron		359
Glencairn		1,647
	Total	5,668

We have the honour to be,

GENTLEMEN,

Your most obedient Servants,

Signed on behalf of the Delegates of the Parishes of Morton, Penpont, Keir, and Tynron,

STEPHEN BROWN, Bennan, Convener.
D. PATERSON, Solicitor, Delegate Secretary.

Thornhill, 30th October, 1896.

Appendix Four

Details of Signalling on the Cairn Valley Railway

The following notes are abridged from a G&SW memorandum issued on 25th February, 1905, which explained the operation of the new Sykes' signalling system.

Sykes' System

The object of this system of working is to prevent more than one train being between any two signal boxes at the same time, as in the case of the Tablet or Electric Staff working, and the locking and signalling have been so laid out that all Passenger trains can only arrive at and depart from the platform lines so that before offering or accepting a passenger train on the block instruments the levers must always be set for these roads.

Goods trains can only arrive on the platform lines but they may be dispatched from the goods yard or loop lines as may be found convenient.

The signalling of trains on this Electric Lock and Block System does not in any way dispense with the use of fixed, hand or detonating signals whenever or wherever such signals may be requisite to protect from obstructions on the line.

The signals are electric disc signals of the same pattern as the shunt signals in use at St Enoch Station.

The danger signal must be kept exhibited at all fixed signals except when it is necessary to lower them for a train to pass.

Fixed Signals at Stations and Intermediate Stations

Each station is provided with home and starting signals for both directions and they are worked by the slides of the block instruments (except the Platform Up Starting Signal at Moniaive and Irongray and the Up Rear Electric Home Signal at Cairn Valley Junction which are worked by a special switch) and not by the ordinary frame levers. There are no distant signals.

No fixed signals are provided for passing to or from the loop lines or sidings (except at Cairn Valley Junction, Irongray and Moniaive) and engine drivers and others concerned must be careful to see that the points leading to and from such loop lines and sidings are in the proper position before allowing trains to pass over them. At Cairn Valley Junction ordinary ground disc signals have been provided and at Irongray and Moniaive there are electrical ground disc signals for controlling trains from the goods loop to the main line.

Working of Fixed Signals

The slide of the block instrument controlling the starting signal to the section ahead, is, after being pulled out, so back-locked that it cannot be replaced to the normal position until the train has passed over the treadle at the station in advance and the signalman there has restored the slide to the normal position and sent the 'Train out of Section' signal. Should however, the necessity arise for a signalman to place a signal at danger before the train reaches the treadle, a switch placed on the shelf in front of the instrument has been provided for this purpose but it does not in any way interfere with the locking or block working.

Working of Apparatus

The slide of the instrument must not be worked quickly or in a jerky manner, but firmly, so as to ensure perfect electrical action inside the instrument and to enable the electric current to do its work properly at both ends of the section; no violence must be used to strain the apparatus nor must the instruments be touched except for the purpose of signalling trains. Signalmen are specially warned that no person, unless specifically authorised, must be allowed to touch the levers or the instruments.

Mode of Signalling

A and B represent each end of a Block Section. The process of signalling is as follows. Before train allowed to start from or pass A, the signalman there (provided he has received 'Train Out of Section' signal for the previous train) must give the 'Is Line Clear?' signal on the ringing key - according to the description of the train - to the signalman at B who must, if the line is clear and he is prepared to receive the train, push in his slide which will automatically lower his home signal (except at Cairn Valley Junction and Irongray - see below) and repeat the block signal on his ringing key and on the last stroke of said signal must hold the ringing key to enable A to withdraw his slide and thus lower A's starting signal, if not prepared to receive he must give one beat.

The signalman at A (after acknowledging the Release by one beat) must on the departure of the train give the 'Train Entering Section' signal which the signalman at B will acknowledge by one beat.

When the train passes over the treadle at the Starting Signal at A, the signal is placed automatically to 'Danger' and it cannot be lowered again to dispatch a following train until the first one has passed out of the section and the starting signal has again been released from B.

When the train has arrived at B and passed over the treadle, B, by putting his slide to the middle or Normal Position will restore his home signal to 'Danger' when he can send the 'Train Out of Section' signal on the ringing key to A and on the last stroke of the said signal he must hold the ringing key for three seconds to enable A to restore his slide to Normal Position and A must then acknowledge it by one beat.

Clearing plunger keys are provided for use when it is necessary to cancel the 'Is Line Clear?' signal previously given and accepted or 'Train Entering Section' signal.

Basically A sends cancelling signal, B repeats, B pushes in No. 2 clearing plunger key which is held in until A pushes in his No. 2 clearing plunger key. B can then restore his slide to Normal Position. B gives one beat acknowledgement on ringing key and holds in for three seconds so A can restore his slide to Normal.

IF THE TRAIN HAS PASSED ON TO OR OVER THE STARTING SIGNAL TREADLE AT A, IT MUST GO THROUGH THE SECTION AND NO CANCELLATION CAN POSSIBLY TAKE PLACE.

Exceptions to Block Working

Irongray Up Starting and Down Home Signals and Up Loop Line Signal cannot be lowered unless the gates of the level crossing are closed across the roadway, as these signals act as gate signals also.

At Cairn Valley Junction in the Up direction the Rear Electric Home Signal cannot be lowered unless the Junction Points are in a position to run the train direct to the main line. This signal is worked by a special switch not by pushing in the slide accepting an Up train from Irongray.

Block Sections

Cairn Valley Junction	-	Irongray
Irongray	-	Newtonairds
Newtonairds	-	Dunscore
Dunscore	-	Moniaive

Crossing of Trains

Crossing of passenger trains approaching from opposite directions, or the shunting of a passenger train for a following passenger train or goods train is prohibited at an intermediate station on a light railway.

Goods trains may be shunted in a loop line for a passenger or goods train to pass.

Goods trains must also (as for all passengers) run into the platform line and thereafter if necessary be shunted into sidings or loop lines as required.

Working of Intermediate Sidings (Stepford, Crossford and Kirkland)

Stepford, Crossford and Kirkland sidings will be worked by down trains only, traffic for Dumfries way being taken to the nearest station in advance and lifted on the return journey. The points of intermediate sidings are controlled by an Annett's key which is kept in a locked box fixed on a post adjoining the ground frame.

After the working of the siding is complete and the points are restored to the normal position the Annett's key must be restored to the instrument in the box and the latter locked, the key of the box being taken by the guard of the train to the next block station ahead and there delivered to the signalman who must return the box key or keys to the signalman at the block station in the rear.

Level Crossings at Birkhall, Irongray, Stepford, Snadeford, Snade Mill and Crossford

Bells are provided in each gate house. When up or down train is warned on the block instrument these ring and an indicating disc shows whether train is up or down. Plunger must be pushed to stop bells and gates closed across roadway.

Cancelled train indicated to the gatekeeper by the bells starting to ring again and disc returning to normal.

Telephonic Communications

Dumfries Telegraph Office	2 beats
Lockerbie Junction	3 beats
Cairn Valley Junction	1 beat pause 2
Irongray	2 beats pause 1
Newtonairds	2 beats pause 2
Stepford	1 beat pause 2 pause 1
Dunscore	1 beat pause 3
Crossford	3 beats pause 1
Kirkland	3 beats pause 2
Moniaive	4 beats
Acknowledgement	1 beat

Working of Steam Motor Carriage

The passenger train service between Dumfries and Moniaive will ordinarily be worked by a steam motor carriage.

Not more than 2 four-wheeled or 2 six-wheeled trailers must be attached.

The engine must be the leading end of the train leaving Dumfries and the Guard's end of the motor carriage must be the leading end of the train leaving Moniaive.

When the Guard's end of the motor is leading and one or two vehicles are attached as trailers, one of the engine drivers must ride in the Guard's compartment of the motor and keep a good look out ahead and be prepared to apply the hand or continuous brake or to sound the engine whistle if necessary to do so.

When one or two vehicles are attached as trailers the Guard must ride in the brake compartment of the rear vehicle. This in no way relieves the driver on the engine of his responsibility for the due observance of signals.

When no vehicles are attached the Guard must keep a good look out and operate the electric bell plunger if necessary to communicate with the driver. He must apply the brakes if necessary.

A bell plunger is provided for the Guard and a bell in the driver's cab.

1 beat	Stop
2 beats	Go forward
3 beats	Go Slowly

The motor carriage must carry one white head light at the leading end and two red side lights and a red tail light in rear.

Acknowledgements

Thanks in particular are due to Stuart Rankin, archivist of the Glasgow and South-Western Railway Association, for inspiration, general support and permission to reproduce his diagrams showing the signalling system and station buildings at Moniaive. I am also very grateful to: the staff of the Scottish Records Office; the Mitchell Library, particularly Murdoch Nicolson; the Ewart Library, Dumfries; and Dumfries Burgh Museum.

Many people also wrote offering information or generously allowed copies of source material to be made. Of these, special mention must be made of: Mrs Alison Maxwell of Edinburgh, granddaughter of station master George Macdonald, for extracts from his, and her father, Douglas Macdonald's, diaries; James Lambie for general advice and for the introduction to Mrs Netta Craig, granddaughter of Moniaive engine driver, Will McConnell; and also Mrs Margaret Anderson who wrote from Sussex with her reminiscences of the railway at the time of World War I. Others who kindly provided source material include James Stevenson, George Robin, John Alsop, Brian Hilton, Ed Nicholls, Henry Corrie, Malcolm Chadwick, Ron Parker, Christine Hiddleston and Ian Henderson, while local memories of the line came from ex-fireman/driver Peter Imrie of Dumfries, and from Moniaive, the late Tom Todd, Sam Todd, Jock Black, James Dykes and Mrs Jean Henderson. The extract in Chapter One from Fergus Paterson's letter was included by kind permission of the James Paterson Museum, Moniaive. Final thanks to David Henderson, who read the manuscript and offered helpful comments.

Card advising the arrival of goods at Kirkland station.   *Jock Black*

Bibliography

Books and Journals

Alexander, A.S., *Tramps Across Watersheds*, John Smith & Son Ltd, 1925.
Barrie, D.S. and Aston, G.J., 'Scottish Light Railways', *Railway Magazine*, January 1936.
Blair-Cunynghame R.O., 'Where Trains Used To Run (Memories of a Branch Line)', Transcript from 1950s BBC Home Service Broadcast.
Corrie, John, Glencairn (Dumfriesshire). *The Annals of an Inland Parish*, Thomas Hunter & Co, Dumfries, 1910.
Cross, Derek, *Roaming The Scottish Rails*, Ian Allan, London, 1978.
Dumfries and Galloway Standard, from 1864.
Engineer, The, 'Steam Motor Carriage, Glasgow and South-Western Railway', 24th March, 1905.
Essery, R. and Jenkinson, D., *An Illustrated History of LMS Locomotives, Volume Three: Absorbed Pre-Group Classes Northern Division*, Oxford Publishing Company, Poole, 1986.
Glasgow and South-Western Railway. Tourist Guide, 1907, John Millar Ltd, Glasgow.
Hawkins C., Reeve G., and Stevenson J., *LMS Engine Sheds, Volume Seven, The Glasgow and South-Western Railway*, Irwell Press, Pinner, Middlesex, 1990.
Highet, Campbell, *The Glasgow & South-Western Railway*, Oakwood Press, 1965.
Kirkpatrick I.J., 'The Cairn Valley Light Railway', G&SWR Association Journals Nos. 21 (1989-90) and 22 (1990-91).
Lindsay Andrew, 'Omnibuses of the Glasgow and South-Western Railway', G&SWR Association Journal No. 16 (1984-85).
LMS Railway Company, *General Appendix, March 1937*.
McAdam, W., *The Birth, Growth and Eclipse of the Glasgow and South-Western Railway*, 1924, Glasgow.
McCarter E.R., 'The Cairn Valley Light Railway', *Railway Magazine* January and February 1944.
Railway Magazine, January 1905, July and August 1943, May and June 1944, September and October 1949, August 1959.
Rankine, W.J., *Dunscore, a Pen Picture of a Country Village*, Dunscore 1975.
Rannie, J.A., 'Dumfries as a Railway Centre', *Railway Magazine*, 1927.
Robin, G.H., 'The Moniaive Branch', G&SWR Association Journal No. 5 (1975-76).
Smith, David L., *Locomotives of the Glasgow and South-Western Railway*, David and Charles, 1976.
Smith, David L., *Tales of the Glasgow and South-Western Railway*, Ian Allan Ltd, 1962.
Smith, David L., 'The G&SWR Rail-Motors', G&SWR Association Journal No. 16 (1984-85).
Stephenson Locomotive Society, *The Glasgow and South-Western Railway 1850-1923*, published by the Society, 1950.
Vallance, H.A., *British Branch Lines*, Batsford, London, 1965.
'The Development of the Railways in South-West Scotland', the *Gallovidian Annual*, 1909, Robert Dinwiddie, High Street, Dumfries.

Archive Material from the Ewart Library, Dumfries

Glencairn Railway Company Prospectus 13th July, 1880.
Report on Navvy Mission - Cairn Valley Railway, 1st September, 1901.

Archive Material from the Scottish Record Office

Glasgow and South-Western Railway Accounts 1905 to 1923.

Glasgow and South-Western Railway, Minutes of Directors' Meetings, 1865 to 1923.

BR/GSW/1/62. G&SW Board Report No. 8, 1896, Memorandum on Moniaive Railway Proposals.

BR/GSW/1/62. G&SW Board Report No. 9, 1896, Memorial to the Directors of the Glasgow and South-Western Railway Company, submitted on behalf of the Parishes of Morton, Penpont, Keir, and Tynron, regarding extension of Line from Thornhill to Moniaive.

BR/GSW/4/10 Page 1. Operating Instructions for the Cairn Valley Railway.

BR/GSW/5/10-(15). Moniaive Steam Motor Working Diagrams.

BR/GSW/24/27. Specification for construction of the Cairn Valley Light Railway.

BR/NBR/4/217 Page 163. G&SW Circular No. 955 regarding opening of the Cairn Valley Railway.

RHP 15390. Plan for Railway from Moniaive to Forrest (Auldgirth) and associated Parliamentary Bill, 1871.

RHP 16995. Plan for Railway from Moniaive to Thornhill, 1896.

RHP 16997. Plan for Station Building at Thornhill for Moniaive to Thornhill Railway.

RHP 30182. Plan for Railway from Moniaive to Dumfries, 1896.

RHP 38329/38. Sketch of proposed Moniaive to Dumfries Railway, 1899.

RHP 43310. Plan for Railway from Moniaive to Forrest (Auldgirth), 1877.

Archive Material from the Public Record Office, Kew

MT29/67. Board of Trade Inspection Report on Signalling Provisions for the Cairn Valley Light Railway, 16th February, 1905.

MT29/72. Board of Trade Inspection Report on New Works Between Stepford and Newtonairds on the Glasgow and South Western Railway, 18th February, 1910.

Archive Material from The James Paterson Museum, Moniaive

MONJP E002-19 F2.2 Letter from Fergus Paterson to his Mother 17th November, 1896.

Parliamentary Papers

Glencairn Railway Bill, 13th November, 1871. (SRO Reference - RHP 43310/3)

Glencairn Railway Act, 6th August, 1872, CH CLXXVI.

Glencairn Railway Act, 27th June, 1881.

G&SW Railway Act, 6th August, 1897, CH CLXXII (Mitchell Library Reference - C342103)

G&SW Railway (Cairn Valley Light Railway) Order 1899.

G&SW Railway Order Confirmation Act 22nd July, 1904 CH CXLII (Mitchell Library Reference - 273438)

Index